A business

Japan

man's guide

Prepared by the Financial Times, London

American
Heritage
Press
New York

Library of Congress Catalog Card Number:
71–109173
SBN: 8281–0094–2

Set in Great Britain by Photoprint Plates Ltd.
in "Monophoto" Times and printed in
Hong Kong by Dai Nippon Printing Co.
(International) Ltd.

Contents

Foreword

Nearly all the economic miracles that have caught the world's imagination at various times since everybody became growth-minded in the early 1950s have long since run into serious difficulties of one kind or another. Yet there is one economic miracle that goes on and on without seemingly needing anything more than an occasional short pause to take breath. It is that for which the energetic and astute Japanese are responsible. And it is worth noting that it has now been going on for so long and at such speed that it has enabled that country to achieve the distinction of being able to lay claim to the second-highest gross national product figure in the Free World.

Yes, in 1968 she came second only to the United States with a total of 142,000 m dollars (£58,000 m). The Japanese had thus already left the hardworking Germans behind, their figure having come out in the same year at 125,000 m dollars (£50,000 m). And there is little doubt that they have since held on to this lead.

In 1968, it is true, the Japanese clocked up a rather higher growth figure than usual, the advance in real terms having amounted to over 14 per cent. But that such attainments are not all that exceptional in a Japanese context may be gauged from the fact that the Japanese gross national product will have rightly quadrupled in the 1960s—which, even allowing for the distortion caused by changes in the purchasing power of money, is quite phenomenal.

Compared with the position obtaining in the early 1950s, when the Japanese were just beginning to throw off the after-effects of their unfortunate participation in World War II, present levels are some eight times higher.

Because of the size of her population—it now numbers over 100 million—Japan's advance to the position of the country with the second-largest output in the Free World does not mean that she has acquired similar eminence in standard of living terms. But her latest massive stride forward has brought her abreast of the least affluent of the advanced countries of West Europe in this sense—Italy and Ireland, for example. And if she continues to outstrip other countries' growth achievements in the way she has been doing during the past few years, it will not be long before she catches up with countries at present located around the middle of the league table like Britain and Belgium.

All kinds of reasons have been put forward for the fact that the Japanese miracle has so convincingly surpassed all others. Almost certainly, however, the main answer lies in the fact that, in the economic field as elsewhere, nothing is apt to succeed so much as success.

To take one illustration of the point, the very fact that production is continually moving ahead so fast makes it much easier for Japan than it is for less progressive countries to cope with the constant pressure for higher wage rates which is a standard feature of the modern scene. And since the rise in consumer expenditure has a hard task in such circumstances to keep pace with the growth of incomes, the savings that are needed to provide the basis for further enlargement of the industrial structure come fairly easily—almost nowhere else in the world is such a high proportion of personal income saved as in Japan.

It used to be said that there was a great deal of similarity, in basic economic circumstances, between Japan and other countries, more especially Britain. If so, the two countries have obviously exploited these circumstances in recent years in signally different fashion.

In the early stages of her advancement from a backward country, Japan was greatly helped by what she learned from the Western nations. People in those countries could obviously profit greatly now by learning from Japan's more recent experiences. It is, probably, too much to suppose that such a resounding success story could ever be repeated in an advanced Western nation. But a careful study of the means the Japanese adopted to get where they are might enable other countries to raise their sights a little higher.

EXPO '70

The Japanese pavilion at EXPO '70 is planned to portray, in the same section as the Forest of Statistics, the Emperor of Japan in a Royal Box, working as a scientist in his own right, among his books on conchology—the science of shells. This image may help to convey the remarkable blend of oriental culture and western technology which is intended to make EXPO '70 at Osaka quite different from its predecessors.

It is meant to be bigger than Brussels 58 and Montreal 67 of course. Its costs are more than double those of Montreal, and it is set among bamboo groves in a bowl in the wooded hills north-east of Osaka, instead of in the middle of the St. Lawrence River. It is also a much more Japanese happening than Montreal was a purely Canadian one. By representing what the Japanese chief architect Kenzo Tange calls the 'model city of the future', it is intended to give the foreign visitor a highly concentrated vision of the results which Japan's supergrowth economy may soon achieve as it pulls abreast of European living standards and gets set to overtake those of North America.

EXPO is designed to put Japan on the world map, thus resolutely contradicting General MacArthur's fatuous remark that it should try to be a 'Far Eastern Switzerland'. It is also meant to build up Osaka on the map of Japan, to rectify the unhealthy concentration of power and population in Tokyo.

Osaka is second only to Tokyo in size, with over 3 million people. It is a business centre with superb modern hotels, sliced up all ways by elevated motorways soaring over the canals, with colourful neon-lit shopping arcades. But from the tourist's point of view, its main attraction is that it is near Kyoto and Nara, Japan's two former capitals, whose temples and shrines were preserved against the wartime bombing by a remarkable victory of the eggheads against the Pentagon.

EXPO '70 is the first world exhibition in the Orient. It is appropriate that Japan should now be getting her chance, in view of the cancellation of the Tokyo exhibition in 1940 by the outbreak of war. But no less than 49 million out of the 50 million visitors expected by the time EXPO closes will be the Japanese them-selves–about half the total population in fact. It thus also serves to bring home to the people of Japan just how advanced their country has become, even if many of them still have to watch their multi-channel colour television in small timber shacks.

Of the one million foreign visitors, 60 per cent are expected to come from North America, 20 per cent from Europe and 20 per cent from the rest of the world, with Asia predominating. Osaka airport has been extended for the new era of the jumbo jets, just in time to handle the enormous EXPO traffic across the Pacific. The travel agencies are able to use the IATA provision for 50 per cent reductions on block bookings, and they commandeered nearly all the available hotel rooms for the first three months from the opening on 15 March.

If the accommodation shortage gets too bad, it is quite feasible to commute the 320 miles from Tokyo on the Hikari (Light) express, which takes just over three hours, and runs every quarter of an hour. It would make a fitting introduction to EXPO, because novel forms of transport are one of the features of this 'model city'. There is the inevitable monorail circling the site. More original are the covered-in air-conditioned moving pavements which can move crowds around at a leisurely pace of just over one mile an hour. For the impatient, there are battery-operated cars or replicas of the famous cable cars provided by San Francisco, Osaka's twin city. Computers are being used to monitor crowd movements and indicate the empty spaces to which people are advised to move.

There are all the usual paraphernalia of any EXPO. An amusement park has nearly three miles of roller coaster track convoluted into an incredibly small space, 146 restaurants with every conceivable national cuisine, a theatre and an art gallery, shopping plazas, and even a new system for tracking down as many as 1,000 children a day who may get separated from their parents.

Work in progress on the EXPO '70 site,
six miles from Osaka.

But the big difference is that the buildings have had to be designed to stand up to the possibility of typhoons of over 100 mph, even though they seldom come earlier than 15 September, the closing day; and to the rainy season, which runs from mid-June to mid-July. There are 10,000 umbrellas for hire, but this is only nibbling at the problem. The most impressive of a variety of new constructional ideas is the roof of the main plaza, which covers the keynote exhibition on the unexceptional theme of 'Progress and Harmony'.

It is a steel frame roof measuring 964 feet by 354, weighing 3,650 tons, which was built on the ground and raised by forty-eight jacks. It is covered by thin cushions of inflated polyester film. A somewhat tasteless looking 'Tower of the Sun' pokes up through the middle, and underneath it, among other things, are two scene-shifting robots 72 feet high, moving on rubber tyres, and equipped with crane arms.

This is but one of many examples of how the Japanese construction industry has acquired, thanks to EXPO, new techniques which should stand it in good stead in other applications. The American pavilion may be taken as a good architectural illustration of what the Japanese call the 'low posture', which is doubtless synonymous with high resistance to typhoons. Costing 10 million dollars (£4.2 m) it is a vast dome—462 feet by 271—of translucent fibre-glass supported on a lattice of steel cables anchored in a concrete rim, and kept in position by compressed air. One tiny sample of moon rock may turn out to be the prize exhibit in this enormous setting.

The Soviet pavilion, at a cost of only 7 m dollars (£2.9 m), is relatively unoriginal, with a 330-foot spike rising out of a steep asymmetrical pyramid. The British pavilion, the first to be completed, combines originality of construction, and orientalism of detail, while remaining strictly functional in keeping with a budget of 4.8 m dollars (£2 m)—only two-thirds that at Montreal. Its main feature is four pairs of orange box girders sticking into the air. Suspended from them above the ground by steel cables are four box-like hangars, walled with steel-faced panels made to look like Japanese shoji paper screen walls.

As there are seventy-seven countries participating, the object of each one has to be to ensure that it is not one of several dozen which will have to be omitted from the tour for lack of time and energy. The French pavilion makes clever use of the compressed air method of construction with four transparent plastic domes, while the German one has such a low posture, whether for meteorological or diplomatic reasons, that it is almost totally underground. The Canadian one has four sloping walls made entirely of mirrors which appear to be made of aluminium, while the State of British Columbia, not to be outdone, has an organ-pipe structure made of giant trees.

The most conspicuous national pavilion is that of Australia, which is almost worthy of the Sydney Opera House in its highly unconventional surrealist flavour. There is a solid structure culminating in a holding arm, which is based on Hokusai's famous print of a wave about to break. Suspended from the arm is a tent shaped structure of cables—this one based on Mount Fuji—from which hangs the circular roof of the entrance to the pavilion. Australia has made a special effort in view of her growing trade with Japan, and will surely succeed in erecting the most talked-about pavilion at Osaka.

But the foreign pavilions have to compete hard to hold their own against the remarkably large number of Japanese ones. Some of the big trusts, or *zaibatsu,* have spent more than some major countries. The Japanese Government of course has the biggest pavilion of all, costing 17 m dollars (£7.1 m). It looks like five drums in shape, but is in fact meant to embody the five-circled cherry blossom EXPO symbol, which in its turn stands for the five continents of the world. (Everything is a symbol of something in Japan.)

The Japanese exhibit is intended to show how this remarkable nation with its Emperor-scientist, manages to keep its ancient culture alive while aiming to lead the world in the application of modern technology. One novelty in the communications field is a map of the world with live television transmissions showing what is happening in each major capital—the ones that are awake at the time, anyway.

Another typical blend of old and new is the Furukawa pavilion, a multi-storey Buddhist pagoda containing a 'Computopia'. The Suntory whisky pavilion mixes cocktails by computer, while Matsushita, the biggest electrical firm, has gone traditional by building a replica of an eighth-century temple set in bamboo groves. The Fuji group has an eye-catching structure of drooping yellow and orange plastic arches filled with air, and Toshiba has a constellation of soaring star-shaped metal tetrahedra. Sanwa screens films all over the inner surface of a dome in a 360 degree arc, and the

Visitors to EXPO '70 will use moving footways such as the one under construction here.

Japan Gas Association has commissioned the Spanish surrealist Miro to carry out a laughter-provoking ceramic mural.

Altogether, the biggest effect of EXPO may be to confirm the Japanese people in the view that their country can now fully hold its own by comparison with anything that the rest of the world can offer. Before the opening, there were 2,000 Japanese visitors a day at the site of the 400-foot observation tower.

EXPO '70 will also help to accelerate Japan's already fantastic rate of growth, and could result in the 12 per cent real expansion of GNP originally forecast for the current financial year ending in March 1970 being raised by as much as 2 per cent. The EXPO authorities themselves budgeted to spend 184.8 m dollars (£77 m) on the basic site facilities and the central exhibits, plus a further 79.2 m dollars (£33 m) on running costs, which should be covered by the 50 million visitors paying a standard fee of 800 yen (just under £1 or 2.4 dollars), though there will be reduced rates, for example for some 10 million Japanese schoolchildren. Another source of income lies in the leases and franchises paid by other exhibitors, who are expected to spend about 300 m dollars (£125 m), altogether. The remaining deficit will be met, one-third by the Osaka local authorities, two-thirds by the central government. To the total of some 564 m dollars (£235 m) must be added about 1,920 m dollars (£800 m) on public works programmes in the whole Osaka area, such as new railways and motorways, and a new town to house 150,000 people just next to the site.

The Japanese are keen to give the impression that their way of life, as it emerges from EXPO '70, is based on traditional cultural values as well as the pursuit of greater material wealth. Perhaps the secret of their success is that they regard the two as insepara-ble. For most of the foreign visitors on their first trip to Japan it will be a revelation of what they have been missing by not coming earlier, in terms of either business opportunities—which a special Expoclub will lay on—or sheer 'Enjoyment of Life', which is the exhibition theme that makes most sense when all the high-minded justifications for such an event are stripped away.

EXPO '70
(From 15 March 1970 to 13 September 1970)

Opening and closing times:
    15 March–28 April

Gates open at	9 30 am
Exhibitions open at	10 00 am
Exhibitions close at	9 00 pm
Gates close at	10 00 pm

    29 April–13 September

Gates open at	9 00 am
Exhibitions open at	9 30 am
Exhibitions close at	9 30 pm
Gates close at	10 30 pm

Daily admission prices:

Adults	800 yen
Youths (15–22 years of age)	600 yen
Children (4–14 years of age)	400 yen

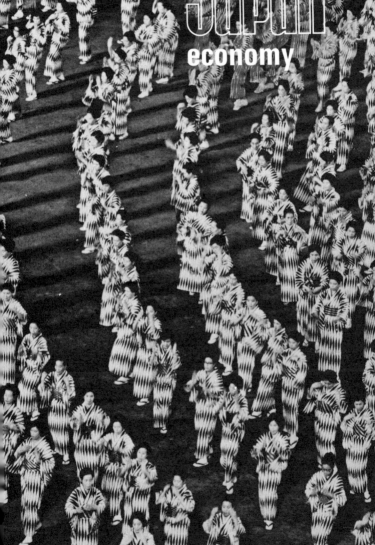

A place in the pattern: the Western cult of the individual is foreign to the Japanese whose loyalties are traditionally to the group. Here, massed dancers perform at a festival.

1

Responsibilities of power

Japan, on the verge of the '70s, is a nation with glowing prospects, and some profound anxieties. The first year of the new decade could be one of the most glorious, or one of the most violent in the country's recent history. It is the year of EXPO '70, the biggest and almost certainly the best international exhibition ever to have been staged in Asia which is to open in Osaka. It is also the year of the coming-of-age and renewal of the ten-year-old US–Japan Security Agreement, an event which could stir up serious trouble inside the country at the very moment when EXPO is getting into its stride.

But the new decade will have another and perhaps still greater significance for Japan and its relations with the rest of the world. During the past year or two the Japanese economic miracle, already familiar for its dynamism and ability to surmount obstacles, has developed a new kind of assurance. Japan today is not only the world's third biggest economy following the United States and Russia, with a rate of growth which promises to make its 100 million people as wealthy as the Americans or the Swedes by 1984. It is also at last becoming a creditor nation, a role which carries responsibilities as well as privileges in the modern world.

Viewed even in purely domestic terms, what has been happening recently has been remarkable enough. During most of its postwar expansion, Japan's economic development has followed what the Japanese themselves like to call the 'walk-run' pattern. That is to say periods of ultra-rapid expansion have been punctuated by phases of slower (though still by European standards very respectable) growth, during which stresses in the balance of payments have been eliminated and the economy has prepared itself for the next upward leap.

The difference between the present phase of expansion and each of its postwar predecessors is that the familiar strains in the balance of payments have not got out of hand. The situation looked serious enough in early 1968 when Japanese foreign exchange reserves slipped below the 2,000 m dollars (£833 m) mark and the Government was doing its best to clamp down the economic brakes. But the result of the measures taken at that time came as a surprise to almost everyone.

Japan's imports during 1968 and the early part of 1969 slowed down to average international levels while the economy as a whole grew faster than ever. With a 24 per cent rise in exports during 1968 and a real increase in the Gross National Product of some 14 per cent, Japan appeared to have freed itself once and for all from the cycle of growth and deficit which up to then had kept Finance Ministry officials in a state of nervous expectancy.

The story of the last half of 1969 was complicated by a rise in internal prices and a modest increase in Bank Rate coupled with some warnings of overheating from the ever-cautious Bank of Japan. But basically the picture remained the same. Japan was still in a state of continuous economic expansion. Foreign exchange reserves were 50 per cent greater than they were at the beginning of 1968 and, barring a serious recession in world trade, there appears no reason why the situation should alter—except for the better.

An analysis of the factors behind this success story

must inevitably fall back on many old and well-tried concepts. There is the famous corporate spirit of the Japanese, the spirit that makes big companies care for their employees with a fatherly concern unequalled anywhere in the West and in return calls forth an impressive quantity of work from the employees. There is the fact that Japanese wage levels are still low by comparison with Europe and the US. (This is so especially if one takes into account the dual economic system under which many large companies rely upon suppliers whose costs—and wage levels—are far lower than their own.)

There is the unrivalled efficiency and modernity of many key sectors of Japanese industry, a heritage in part of wartime destruction but also of the Japanese determination in the postwar period to buy and put to work the very best the rest of the world had to offer in technical and managerial know-how. Finally, and perhaps most important, there is the rate of capital investment, which for most of the past fifteen years has been higher in Japan than anywhere else in the industrial world.

This last clue to the Japanese economic miracle has been more significant than ever in the very recent past. As a result largely of deliberately introduced Government incentives, there was an increase of no less than 33 per cent in private capital investment by the most rapidly expanding sectors of Japanese industry in 1967 and of 22 per cent in 1968, causing capacity to be created which in the following years could only be channelled into exports. But given the fact that the miracle has occurred—and seems to be continuing—there is also the question of what the Japanese are going to do about it. Does the country's new-found wealth combined with its traditional dynamism mean simply that everything will go on as before, only more so? Or does it herald a change in Japan's traditional posture in world affairs?

In certain rather technical fields, particularly those

5

concerned with foreign exchange and the balance of payments, there are already signs of change. Japan's heavy dependence on short-term borrowing in the US and on the Eurodollar market has significantly lessened, under the process which the Japanese Press has christened the 'yen shift' and which involves, in essence, the allocation of a bigger share of trade financing to the country's domestic banks. Attitudes to overseas investment by the Finance Ministry and the Bank of Japan have softened, with effects that have quickly become noticeable in some capital-importing countries. Japanese investment in Australia and New Zealand is now a factor to be reckoned with and could be crucial to the success of such projects as the huge Robe River iron ore project in Western Australia or the expansion of the coal and bauxite industries in Queensland. But these and other developments represent only the first phases of what could become a whirlpool of economic reorganisation. Economists at Japan's two most prestigious universities of Tokyo and Kyoto have been talking about the situation which might arise when foreign exchange reserves reach 5,000 m dollars (£2,083 m) and Japan, like West Germany, starts to be faced with the problems of a permanently growing surplus. Some have concluded there is no alternative to a revaluation of the yen. To others the outlook seems less alarming, but perhaps also more challenging.

Of the many steps which Japan's overseas trading partners would like to see her take the foremost is import liberalisation. Japan maintains import restrictions on a total of 120 items which are freely traded in most other parts of the world and should, according to the letter of GATT, be free in Japan also. The derestriction of such items and the elimination of some of the surviving peaks in the Japanese tariff system would be a difficult political exercise for the Liberal Democrat Government. It is no secret that many of the items concerned are agricultural and the Liberal Democrat Party has always leant heavily on rural support. However, liberalisation would pay dividends in terms of international (and particularly American) goodwill. It is likely to be taken up with some urgency in the next year or so by the Japanese Government. Indeed, it is possible that at least half the current range of import controls may have been withdrawn by the end of 1971.

The other topic to which the Japanese are being urged to address themselves, and which many people within Japan are now taking very seriously, is foreign aid. Few would dispute that Japan now has the resources to lend (or even give) more money to its needy South-east Asian neighbours and many would argue that it is directly in the interests of Japan to do so. Japan's chances of remaining a highly competitive trading nation probably lie in continued exposure to the products of the developing world (particularly those members of it which, like Korea, Taiwan and Singapore are beginning to climb the industrial ladder). To assist these nations to survive and prosper Japanese aid could prove indispensable.

There are of course more specific reasons why as time goes on Japan is likely to become increasingly preoccupied with events in South-east Asia. The stability of the area is vital to Japan's own prosperity, even perhaps to its survival since the all important shipping route to Europe and the Middle East passes through the straits of Malacca between Indonesia and Singapore. But for the time being there is only one weapon which Japan can effectively use to promote its interests outside its own borders, given the limited size of its defence forces and the pacifist nature of its constitution. This weapon is economic power. It will become progressively more formidable during the coming decade.

2

The persistent miracle

Japan, which kept 81 million people going on a gross national product of 7,200 m dollars (£3,000 m) in 1949, maintained 102 million in a comparatively advanced state of comfort on a GNP of around 162,800 m dollars (£67,000 m), in 1969. The country's seemingly over-ambitious income-doubling plan for 1961–70 reckoned on a GNP of 72,000 m dollars (£30,000 m) by the end of the decade, so it's distinctly 'old hat'. The plan was really only a marshalling of available facts and factors—'What would be a long-range economic plan for a stable development of the Japanese economy?' was the one-sentence term of reference from the then Prime Minister Kishi to his Economic Deliberation Council—and it had to be revised upwards within two or three years when it became obvious that Japan's growth was going to be on a scale never envisaged by older in-dustrial countries for themselves. Even West Germany's miracle would take second place.

Most of us find Japan's frequently quoted '10 per cent growth a year for the past ten years' impressive enough, but in fact it was 14·3 per cent in real terms in fiscal 1968, following 13·3 per cent in fiscal 1967. The result for 1969 may fall a bit below those figures, owing to persistently rising prices, but Japanese planners feel confident enough to peer into the distant years and tell us what to expect in 1975. Less inhibited forecasters see 1985 clearly in the crystal ball.

Take the Japan Economic Research Centre. It will not be surprised if the economy advances by 11·5 per cent a year in real terms between 1970 and 1975, but this is only a shade more than the 11·1 per cent a year through the 1960s. The estimated GNP of 192,960 m dollars (£80,400 m) in fiscal 1970 will have become 418,000 m dollars (£174,200 m) by fiscal 1975. This takes Japan's *per capita* GNP from 1970's 1,848 to 3,778 dollars (£770 to £1,574) in 1975—with a leap from seventeenth to ninth among the well-to-do nations. For comparison, Britain's 2,023 dollars (£843) *per capita* which would give her fifteenth place in 1970 would progress to 2,626 dollars (£1,094) and sixteenth place in 1975.

The splendidly-named 'National Over-all Development Council' is one of the Prime Minister's several happy bands of prognosticators. It has told him that the Prime Minister in office in 1985 can expect to control the destinies of 120 million people in 35·5 million families, and that the GNP will be 418,000 m dollars (£174,000 m). This latter figure is forecast for 1975 by the Japan Economic Research Centre. The National Over-all Development Council foresees a growth rate of only 8 per cent a year over the two decades 1965–85, which seems likely to prove an underestimate. Accumulated capital investment during the twenty-year period will be worth 1,387,200 m dollars (£578,000 m), or something like four times the total for the whole of Japan's first century of modernity (1868–1968).

By then, Japan will have converted itself into a 'new industrial society' suited to the computer, superjet age, with a vast network of trunk roads and railways bolstering her economic growth. By then, too, it seems that even the industrious Japanese might indulge in a little more leisure—the planners say '1·4 times more in 1985 than 1965', thanks to reduced working hours. There will be millions fewer working at farming, forestry and fishing, but millions more will have joined the ranks of the white collar workers. What of the 'blue collars' who now man the assembly lines? It can only be assumed that there will be a computer standing at the end of each assembly line, making sure that automation is putting the nuts and bolts in the right places.

Road complex, built originally for the
1964 Olympic Games.

In this 1965–85 era, there is also going to be a determined effort to break up the present concentration of industry and population around Tokyo and Osaka, through relocating industrial plants in remote areas (it is the present state of Japan's communications that prevents this development). The cities will abound with tall buildings, avers the National Over-all Development Council, housing the people as well as the offices. The dimension of this problem may well be judged from these simple facts: there were 22 million people in Tokyo and surrounding areas at the last count, and that was 21·6 per cent of the national population. By

The Oi head office of the Daiichi Life Insurance Company in country surroundings opened up by the Tokyo-Nagoya Speedway.

3

A supergrowth society

Japan is now advancing at twice the speed of any other industrial economy. Even more remarkable, she has every chance of continuing to notch up annual economic growth rates in double figures, of anything between 10 and 14 per cent. Like a space-ship which has left the pull of the earth's gravity, she seems to have reached a state of high-speed inertia, in which it is easier to maintain the self-sustaining process of rapid economic growth than to imagine any external forces which could seriously impede it.

Other countries have instruments of economic management similar to Japan's, without approaching her growth record, so she must have something more that they lack. Nor can her performance any longer be written off as a temporary spurt to catch up with the more advanced countries who did not suffer such devastation in the war, since she is now overtaking them a quarter of a century after Hiroshima. The explanation of Japan's economic success lies deeper than economic causes alone. It is also to be found in the very structure of Japanese society.

The Japanese national character is peculiarly suited to the country's economic sense of mission. To a far greater extent than Britain itself, it embodies the old English virtue of 'team spirit'. The Japanese have developed the art of working in groups while at the same time giving the individual scope to develop his talents. These group loyalties may operate at the level of the corporation, of the industry, or of the nation as a whole, in its competition against other nations. As a shrewd American observer put it: 'You see these little men running around the field, then suddenly they all run the same way, and wham! they've run off with the goalposts.'

This 'team spirit' is sometimes attributed to the homogeneity of the Japanese as a race, which was for many centuries cut off from contact with the outside world in its islands. Perhaps even more important is the educational system, which helps to ensure that the hierarchies which still undoubtedly exist are based on merit, searchingly tested by examinations, rather than on social class. As many as 70 to 80 per cent of the school population now stay on to complete high school courses until eighteen, and as many as 55 per cent of those who stay on at school go on to college of some kind. Built into this system is a bias towards technology and economics, which ensures that the top graduates compete for places by examination in Japan National Railways or Mitsubishi, often as their first preference.

Economic growth has become the top national objective, and political issues have become subordinate to it. But the Japanese economic system resembles neither Soviet communism nor Western capitalism. It has the dynamism of capitalism but attempts to eliminate both the uncertainties of risk-taking and the wastefulness of excessive competition. It also succeeds, where communism has vainly tried, in persuading the individual to harness his efforts to the furtherance of society's interests in such a way that he ultimately benefits far more than if he followed his own inclinations.

Japan, as befits the leading country of the 'third world', seems to have discovered what Harold Macmillan once called the 'middle way' between capitalism and communism. Perhaps its most important single economic feature is the high rate of gross fixed investment, which is running at about one-third of gross national product. This expression of confidence by industrial corporations in future growth prospects is based on a number of factors peculiar to Japan.

First, political stability. Unlike two-party states such as Britain and the United States, where a change of party at elections may mean a change of economic policy, Japan has one governing party, the Liberal-Democratic Party, which has a virtual monopoly of power, and changes only its personalities and its emphasis from time to time. The result of a general election thus brings little change in the investment climate.

Second, government support for business. Any firm which takes a risk by borrowing to the hilt in order to invest in a new technological process can be fairly sure that the authorities, acting as they do through the banking system, will help it to tide over any short-term financial crisis—as in the case of Sanyo Steel in 1965. This does not on the other hand apply to the smaller backward firms which get into difficulties through failure to modernise.

Third, the separation of control and ownership in major industries. The men who manage Japanese business are seldom gambling with their own money when they launch their grandiose new investment projects. There is not even much of a risk for the shareholders, because equity is such a small proportion of total capital resources, and bank loans such a large one. On the other hand, the top managers do get rewards, in terms of salary, fringe benefits and promotion as their corporation increases in size and importance. Their aim is to increase turnover rather than short-term profits, but they assume, with some justification, that long-term profits will benefit as their corporation's market share increases.

Fourth, the constant union pressure for higher wages at a time of labour shortage. In any other country, this might be the red light signal to put up the defences against inflation by slowing down the pace of growth. In Japan, it is a stimulus to invest even more in new equipment, with the most modern technology the world has to offer, and to shift resources from labour-intensive industries such as textiles into capital-intensive ones such as information. This raises productivity enough to justify annual wage increases of the order of 10 per cent in real terms, and remedies the shortage of labour. But it would be impossible without

Perfume: one of the many displays of Western products seen in the vast department stores of Tokyo.

the group loyalty and high educational standards which form part of the social structure.

To give an example of this philosophy of high investment, one of Japan's top steel men gave what he regarded as a somewhat conservative view, that steel-making capacity should continue, as in the past, to add 15 million tons to its capacity every two years, thus raising production from just over 80 million tons in 1969 to 110 million tons in 1973. The optimum output for the new steel plants now being planned is 12 million tons each.

It should not be imagined that this kind of investment programme is based on some kind of gamble about export market opportunities. With 100 million people, Japan has one of the world's biggest and most concentrated home markets, which is the main basis for her economic strength. Exports still account for only just over one-tenth of GNP, less than in most of her European competitors. Her success abroad is as yet modest by the standards of her economic potential, and is the consequence rather than the cause of her economic miracle. (Foreigners often make the mistake of thinking that the men who matter in Japanese business are always the ones who speak good English.)

Japan's almost incidental—to her—success in foreign markets is both a problem and an opportunity. It is a problem because her reserves, now about 3,000 m dollars (the exact figure depends whether you count in the IMF contribution), are expected to rise to 4,700 m dollars by the end of 1970, and to something like 10,000 m dollars by 1975, if present trends continue. It is an opportunity because it makes possible an even faster rate of economic growth designed to whittle down the trade surplus, and an even more rapid liberalisation of trade and payments control than the rather leisurely stage by stage affair originally intended.

Japan will go to great lengths to avoid a revaluation of the yen. She is already employing some of the same arguments that the Germans used to cite against revaluation, such as saying that the weak currencies should adjust downwards, not the strong ones upwards. But her situation is different. Her reserves are not all that substantial by German standards; her exchange control is still tight enough to keep speculation in favour of the yen at bay, with the purchase of Japanese securities offering the only way in for foreign operators; and she would be justified in asking the world to wait and see the effects of trade and payments liberalisation on her surplus before taking the extreme step of un-hitching the yen from the dollar to which it is so closely tied.

The ending of import quotas, of which the most serious are on processed foods and agricultural produce, would benefit Japan as well as the rest of the world. It would cut back her payments surplus by some 500–1,000 m dollars a year, help to check rising food prices by bringing in cheap imports, and relieve industry's labour shortage by reducing the high proportion of 19 per cent of the population still living on the land. The rest of the world would benefit by the opening of a major new farming market. If Australia and New Zealand could sell more butter and lamb in Japan, the entry of membership candidates into the European Common Market would be greatly eased.

Unfortunately, the Japanese Government, like so many others, sets great store by political support from the farmers, who will not take kindly to this plan. There is also the specially Japanese difficulty over land use. The most productive farming land, which should remain viable even after imports have been freed, lies in the coastal plain, and is being competed for by industry. The Japanese authorities, never at a loss, therefore have a plan to decentralise industry so that the proportion in the Tokyo–Nagoya–Osaka corridor would fall from 30 to 10 per cent by 1980.

The other way of working off the payments surplus would be by liberalising outgoing investment. There has already been some relaxation of control over direct foreign investment by Japanese corporations, which is natural enough in view of Japan's wish to increase her aid programme in Asia. But the authorities seem relatively reluctant to allow Japanese portfolio investors to buy foreign shares, on the grounds that a country's savings should be for its own use, and not that of others.

Liberalisation of the economy, though long overdue if Japan is to conform to the rules of the international game, will not necessarily mean the end of the surplus. It may not be carried far enough, or it may only be executed in return for counter-concessions in favour of Japanese exports whose net effect is actually to increase the surplus. In that case, we may hear more of the argument that the yen should be revalued, although the Japanese authorities tend to think that the question will not really arise until the mid-1970s.

Japan's best way of keeping the surplus to manageable proportions will be to continue to expand her own economy at the rate of 12 per cent or so, rather than the more cautious figure of 2 or 3 per cent less favoured by some of her bankers. One way of bringing this about will be for the Government to press on with the current increase in its own investment programme, so as to make up the lag in areas such as housing, roads, and social security, which have taken second place to the expansion of industrial investment. Housing expenditure has recently been rising at an annual rate of 30 per cent already.

The Japanese, in a typically 'low posture' argument, sometimes point out that their rapidly rising GNP per head figures gives a misleading impression, because Japan comes lower down the scale in any international comparison of accumulated capital wealth per head. But if the current rate of investment continues, and is channelled more in the direction of public welfare, Japanese wealth per head will soon catch up with Western standards too. How long will it take the other countries of Asia to catch up with Japanese standards?

4

Foreign investment barriers

Foreign investment has long been something towards which the Japanese have had an ambivalent attitude. Such investment is welcome in that it helps the balance of payments and also marks foreign confidence in Japan, but on the other hand the Japanese do not like foreign businessmen running companies where Japanese management could do as well.

Such a nationalistic attitude towards foreign investment is met with in many countries. The Japanese have been, in very rough terms, as restrictive as any other Asian country, and a lot tougher than any European country, including France. Gradually, however, the Japanese are being obliged to liberalise investment, under strong pressure from the West.

Before the war a limited number of foreign companies penetrated deep into the Japanese economy; among these were the international oil companies and also some electrical firms. Their advantage was technical knowledge, and they made breaches in Japanese defences that were never repaired. Today foreign capital is strongest in the oil industry; Shell, the largest foreign investor in Japan, has kept a slowly shrinking but important share of the domestic oil market.

In addition to the oil companies specialised firms— IBM and Coca-Cola, for instance—acquired 100 per cent subsidiaries in Japan. On the whole, however, it has been impossible since the war for a foreign company to set up a 100 per cent operation in Japan and there have been a mass of restrictions preventing foreign interests from obtaining majority interest companies in Japan.

This is, in practice, still almost the position today. In principle Japan has taken some very important steps towards liberalisation of direct investment in the past few years; and the authorities have also approved the formation of a limited number of 100 per cent foreign owned companies. At the same time the controls on investment in most really interesting areas are still hard or impossible to beat. There have been several duels between the Japanese authorities and foreign— mostly American—companies in the past few years. So far, the former have won.

It was in 1966 that the Japanese first announced that capital liberalisation would take place—under pressure from the OECD and also the United States and European countries. The Japanese idea was that liberalisation might also benefit Japan; and such organisations as Keidanren, the leading businessmen's association, came out in favour of liberalisation from this 'positive' point of view. By June 1967 those concerned with capital liberalisation—in the three leading Ministries and Keidanren—had worked out their views on the future of capital liberalisation. Only one Ministry, the Ministry of International Trade and Industry, was really out of line, displaying the protectionist attitude for which it is well known.

MITI was, however, obliged to modify its views, and the first round of capital liberalisation since the war was announced in July 1967, with much publicity. The Japanese view was that great concessions had been made; altogether fifty industries were being liberalised —seventeen industries were totally freed and another 33 per cent were opened up to 50 per cent foreign joint ventures. In principle, this did mark a great departure—

as 100 per cent liberalisation had hitherto been almost unthinkable; but in practice the programme paved the way for very little action. There were very few possible applications for investment in Japan following this first round of liberalisation, as the liberalised industries were all ones in which Japan was very strong—steel and shipbuilding, for instance.

The Japanese Government was well aware of the disappointment among foreign business people, and a month after the announcement of the first liberalisation round, the authorities stated that most industries should be liberalised by about 1970; a 'negative list' of those industries which would not be freed would be established. Meanwhile MITI, reluctant to admit defeat, announced its own formal position that there might be an increase in the number of industries subject to 50 per cent liberalisation, but that the 100 per cent liberalised industries should not become too numerous. Once again the protectionists were to be beaten.

In the autumn of 1968 Prime Minister Eisaku Sato announced that capital liberalisation would be more rapid in future, one indication that the broadminded element in the Japanese business world had finally won the day. Early in 1969 virtually all industries said that capital liberalisation would be possible eventually—with the exception of the obstinate automobile industry. The second round of liberalisation took place in March 1969, when an additional 142 industries were put in the 50 per cent liberalised list, and another twenty-eight were made 100 per cent free. So about one-third of Japanese industry had been liberalised to some degree; and yet the most interesting sectors still remained protected.

The most important round of liberalisation will inevitably be the last one, but before that stage there will be a third round of intermediate liberalisation. This is expected to take place in the autumn of 1970, with the fourth and final round at the end of fiscal 1971, or about March 1972. So Japanese business is being given plenty of time to put its house in order before the 'invasion' of capital, as the Japanese Press sometimes call it.

The prospect is that most of Japanese industry will be liberalised by March 1972, and yet one would not expect an inrush of foreign capital. There are certain fields, where foreign know-how may be vastly superior to Japanese; but these limited areas are likely to remain protected. On the whole, Japanese business will remain very Japanese, and the scope for foreign firms to capture important new positions will be rather small.

The US, in other words, will find it hard to do in Japan what she has accomplished in Europe. Equally European business may be thwarted, though in some cases Europeans will be able to take advantage of Japanese fears of 'giant' American capital, and slip in ahead of US competitors.

5

Exchanging knowhow

The outstanding strength of Japanese industrial research is in the field of development and applications. In regard to basic research most Japanese manufacturing concerns are still lagging behind their counter-members in the Western highly industrialised countries, even if this gap has been narrowing during the last few years.

During the postwar period, Japanese authorities were encouraging Japanese manufacturers to buy processes and 'knowhow' from Western factories in order to overcome as quickly as possible the technological gap which had become prominent during the war, when Japanese industries were cut off from the main stream of scientific and industrial progress in the West.

The buying of technology was a quicker and more effective way to modernise Japanese industries than to rely on research work to be carried out in Japanese laboratories and factories. At the same time Japanese industrial research was able to be devoted to further developments of advanced technology which was bought from leading industrial firms of the West. This policy has paid off handsomely for Japan's industrial development, and Western firms who have entered into agreements with Japanese manufacturers have also benefited by these arrangements. Some Western manufacturers who signed their first agreements in the 'fifties have since extended their technological cooperation with their Japanese partners, which clearly indicates the satisfactory working of these arrangements for all parties concerned.

The Western firms were able to reap the benefits of participating in the rapidly expanding economy of a country with an internal market of 100 million population, the buying power of which has been rising at a high rate. It was, and still is, easier to supply some markets in the Far East (for example, South Korea, Taiwan) from Japanese factories than from Europe. In addition to earning royalties from such arrangements, Western firms had the advantage of exporting during the introductory period these products from their own factories to Japan. There are also other advantages of such cooperation with manufacturers of the highly industrialised Japan, which is situated about 10,000 miles away from Europe. In the case of plant and machinery in certain cases it has proved to be a satisfactory arrangement to ship intricate components from the United States or Western Europe to be built into equipment manufactured by Japanese factories.

There are several instances when German and Swiss machinery and equipment manufacturers who, because of a too long backlog of orders, were supplying their European and overseas customers with products from their Japanese licensees.

A leading European firm of electrical machinery makers which has been licensing its products to a prominent Japanese manufacturer for many years, reports that on various occasions its Japanese partners have come up with valuable suggestions on improvement (further development) of the products and of the production process, which were then incorporated in the European plant.

Technological skill in leading Japanese manufacturing factories is very high. Laboratories of these factories are equipped with most up-to-date instruments. The emphasis is on team work, and the large number of university graduates, many of whom have a PhD degree, employed by Japanese industrial concerns in their central research institutes and also in laboratories attached to their individual plants (coupled with highly sophisticated equipment—the installation of which is not only due to the gadget-mindedness of the Japanese) is one of the basic explanations of the thrust and success of Japanese science-based industries. The contact between universities and industry is stronger than in Western Europe.

The very well equipped laboratories provide ample scope for Japanese scientists to work in their own country. The majority of Japanese university graduates who go to work abroad return to Japan after a few years (contrary to European highly skilled migrants who settle, for example, in the US). The experience and knowledge acquired by young Japanese scientists and technologists abroad becomes after their return to Japan a great asset to them, their employers, and Japan's overall economy.

The trend towards science-based industries is very pronounced in Japan. Professor D. H. Chorafas refers in his book, *The Knowledge Revolution,* to the Japanese success in shipbuilding, and gives the following details of the manufacture of micro-computers: 'Thirty-five firms around the world have thrust into this field. Of these fifteen are European, eight are American and twelve are Japanese. But if integrated circuits are taken as a typical example, no European firm is involved, while four American and nine Japanese firms are the forerunners. The Japanese outpace the Americans by more than two to one.' He makes the assessment that: 'If the last twenty years have been those of the American challenge in Europe, the coming twenty years promise to be the years of the Japanese challenge.'

The future will show how far this assessment is correct. However, the fact is that the industrial developments in Japan have already led to the technological cooperation between Japanese and Western manufacturers consisting of *exchange* of processes and know-how, that is, in twoway licensing arrangements, contrary to the postwar period practice when only Western processes were licensed to Japanese firms.

An interesting example is the production process for urea. The Dutch company DSM has licensed its Stamicarbon process to Mitsubishi Petrochemical, whereas the process developed by Toyo Koatsu (which later became Mitsui Toatsu) was licensed to ICI in Britain and to BASF in Germany.

During the postwar period US firms were the main suppliers of technological know-how to Japanese manufacturers, and other European firms were also very active in this field. British firms, with a few notable exceptions, badly neglected valuable opportunities which existed in Japan at that time.

In the British motor car industry Rootes (Hillman cars) and Austin had entered into technological agreements (with an initial supply of knocked-down cars, then switching over to complete local production) with Japanese manufacturers.

In the chemical industry ICI saw early the advantages of cooperation with leading Japanese companies, and has licensed to Sumitomo Chemical the technology to produce low density polyethylene (production started 1958) and other products, including polymethyl methacrylate (1967). The technology to produce Terylene fibre was licensed to Toyo Rayon Company (1957). The ICI steam reforming gas process is used by Japanese gas companies (engineered by Humphreys and Glasgow and Power Gas, both contractors who have been very active in Japan). Sumitomo Chemical use the ICI-Kellogg naphtha reforming process in their ammonia plant at Nihama. These are just a few highlights of ICI operations in Japan.

The Anglo-Dutch concern, Shell, is very successful in their activities in Japan and among their operations is close cooperation (including financial participation) with Mitsubishi Petrochemical. BP have granted a licence to Kyowa Hakko to produce synthetic protein from oil.

The trend of Japanese industrial successes, coupled with the rising standard of living of the Japanese population, provides new opportunities for licensing new products and technology to Japanese firms as well as for securing new technology from Japanese manufacturers.

6

Labour in demand

When a Japanese school-leaver or university graduate takes a job he virtually decides the course of his professional career and to a large extent his social life for the next thirty or forty years, since it is assumed by both worker and employer that the acceptance of a job is a commitment for life or until retirement, usually at fifty-five. Of course, many people throughout the world prefer to stay with one company for their working life, but it is only in Japan that such a practice has become firmly established and universally accepted.

In return for loyalty to his company, the average Japanese worker receives not only security of employment, but a wide range of fringe benefits and welfare facilities—in addition to twice-yearly bonuses, which often amount to three or four months' salary and which are regarded as part of wages. Benefits commonly extended include health insurance and pension schemes, family allowances, educational facilities, discount stores, housing or housing allowances, free excursions and sometimes even holidays. Female workers can often attend classes to learn flower arrangement, cooking and the art of the tea ceremony.

Sports are widely catered for; most major firms run teams, some of which win national acclaim. Kajima Construction Company are famous in Japan for their baseball team, Yawata Iron and Steel excel at soccer, while Riccar Sewing Machine Company boast a crack athletics team. In fact, a women's volleyball team from Nichibo, the textile people, won a gold medal for Japan in the 1964 Tokyo Olympics.

Executives do not receive all the benefits given to workers, but they are adequately compensated by such perks as membership of exclusive golf clubs, lavish expense accounts and visits to night clubs financed by their company.

Apart from paternalism, Japan's employment system is characterised by wage structures related to length of service and educational background rather than to ability or productivity. The great capitalists, who at the end of the last century laid the foundations of Japan's industrial growth, combined modern business methods with the belief that length of service was synonymous with ability, and this belief still holds sway today.

Labour mobility is low; anyone changing jobs runs the risk of being considered unstable by prospective employers, who would assume that he could only have left his job because of a serious misdemeanour. However, traditions are slowly changing. Mobility has been increasing of late and more and more enterprises are introducing wage rates based on efficiency.

By far the main cause of change is shortage of labour. Though Japan has a labour force of roughly 51 million the country is acutely short of skilled and young workers. Many firms are finding that they are unable to implement schemes to expand production simply because they lack the necessary staff.

Ten years ago industry managed to meet its man-power needs with relative ease, but in recent years, and especially since 1965, demand has far exceeded supply. During 1968, job openings rose 8 per cent, but total employment increased only 3·1 per cent. At one time in 1969 there was one junior high-school leaver for every 4·9 jobs and one senior high-school leaver for every 5·7 vacancies. What is more, all the estimates and surveys agree that shortages will become even more serious in the future. It has been predicted that 1970 junior high-school leavers will number 18 per cent fewer than 1969 and senior high school leavers 8 per cent fewer.

To cope with labour shortages company personnel officers have had to widen their hunting grounds to take in part-time and older workers and married women. Heavy industries are even beginning to employ women for manual tasks; Ishikawajima-Harima Heavy Industries, for instance, has fifty women working in its Yokohama shipyard. Management in Japanese factories

Office girls attend a class in the art of the tea ceremony, one of many sponsored by their company.

has had to dream up new schemes to attract labour. Tokyo Shibaura Electric (Toshiba) aroused comment several years ago by wooing more than 700 girls into its factories with free flights to Tokyo. Similar practices have not gone unnoticed by the Japanese Ministry of Labour, which in 1968 had cause to reprimand 800 employers for engaging in 'excessive' activity in trying to lure job applicants.

Labour shortages have contributed much towards rapidly increasing wages. A study of the wage advances resulting from the annual 'Spring Offensive'—the traditional drive for better wages—shows that wages rose by an average 10 per cent a year over the period 1955 to 1965, by 12 per cent in 1967, by 14·2 per cent in 1968, and by 15 per cent in 1969. In the previous year incidentally, the average monthly wage of employees of firms with more than thirty workers was 55,405 yen (about 155 dollars or £64).

In view of the widespread labour shortage it is surprising that companies still persist in retiring workers at fifty-five. The practice went unquestioned when life expectancy was not much higher and when Japan enjoyed an abundance of young workers, but now that expectancy has reached sixty-eight for men and seventy-three for women (on a par with European levels), retirement at fifty-five is an anomaly. Some firms have already raised retirement age, but they are in the minority. If more companies followed their example it would obviously go a long way towards alleviating the problems caused by shortages of labour. Approximately 35 per cent of employed persons are members of trade unions, most of them organised on a single-industry basis and linked in a federal structure. The largest federation is the General Council of Japanese Trade Unions (SOHYO). This is affiliated with the Japan Socialist Party and draws a high proportion of its membership from the government and public corporations fields. It is now making virtually no gains in membership. The leadership still uses Marxist doctrine and rhetoric, but the rank-and-file, being fairly conservative and concerned mainly with economic gains, is apathetic or increasingly hostile to continued political activity. The Japan Confederation of Labour (Domei) is making considerable progress, especially in organising workers in private industry. Domei supports the Democratic Socialist Party and is willing to work with management on productivity plans, the automation problem and modernisation of plants. Soka Gakkai, the militant Buddhist sect to which the Komeito party is affiliated has launched an effort to organise its own labour federation, but it is still too early to say what the results will be. The drive is aimed at workers mainly in small and medium businesses, now unorganised.

The main employers' group handling labour relations is the Japan Federation of Employers' Associations.

Federation and labour groups have semirecognised status with the government and are represented on advisory bodies. The government does not intervene in strikes or other labour troubles except to handle those which involve unions in the government, public corporation and transport sectors. Strikes usually do not continue for more than a few days at most and very often are only hours long.

7

Managers of Japan

The Japanese system of lifelong employment, for managers and workers alike, often causes mystification in Western countries. How, asks a Western manager, can a company get by with *not ever* laying off workers and axing a few managers? It is often assumed that the Japanese system must be a hangover from a previous and more feudal era, and be a negative feature of Japanese industry that must, surely, soon be abandoned.

But this is to look at it with Western eyes. In fact, as applied to blue-collar workers, the 'lifelong employment' system has only been widely applied since the war, although it certainly does owe its origin to much older Japanese social traditions. Even for white-collar workers, it only dates back to the 1920s. What is more, given Japan's sharp division between big companies and small companies, the system only applies to the big company sector. But without doubt the relation of mutual obligation which it implies carries tangible benefits for Japanese industry. For the employer on the one hand accepts the obligation to keep his workers in employment, and will cut dividends rather than dismiss them—with the full approval of creditors and stockholders. The worker, on the other hand, values the *status of being employed* by the company, rather than the specific job or job content. So he accepts a general obligation to do all he can to make the company prosper. The basic concept is that of a clan—a social as much as a business community.

This has several consequences. Strikes tend to be of short duration *except* in those unusual cases where employers have tried to dismiss workers. Second, a Japanese worker is far more flexible than his Western counterpart, far more ready to change jobs or job methods, just because the idea of job property rights is quite absent in Japan. Hence also the absence of demarcation disputes. Japanese workers will, if necessary, take pay cuts to keep the company going, provided the management is also making sacrifices. Similarly, the system of regular individual annual wage increases for everyone, white and blue-collar, based on age and number of years of service, and quite separate from union-negotiated across-the-board increases, is a recognition of the fact that a man, first and foremost, pledges his life's work to the company, and is only secondarily employed for a particular job.

As a corollary, a man who changes jobs by going to another employer is apt to be regarded with suspicion in Japan, as being unstable and unreliable. Conversely, a man is not fired for incompetence, merely transferred to work where he can do less damage. Another corollary of the system is that piece rates simply do not exist in Japan.

The inability to declare redundancies has caused embarrassment in certain declining industries, notably coal mining. But in general it has undoubtedly helped to create relatively peaceful labour relations (after the massive wave of strikes immediately postwar), and has given managers the security and identification with the company needed by their class everywhere. Also, the degree of immobility must not be exaggerated. The big Japanese companies are really loose confederations of many different companies. Transfer of workers can and does take place within each confederation, in response to surpluses and shortages. This type of transfer *within* the clan is quite acceptable, and means that there is some 'hidden' mobility in the system. It is also in order to transfer people to subcontractors who have close relations with the main company, and who are in a sense part of the clan.

The system also accounts for the union organisation of Japan. Because each company is to be regarded as a social unit, with strong internal loyalties, it is natural to base unions on the company, rather than on the industry or the skill. In Japan the company union is a natural product of the country's traditions, and means that each union is clearly identified with the success (or failure) of its company, just as are the workers in the company in their individual capacities. Unions in Japan are certainly not subservient. But neither do they have the century-old tradition of conflict with the employers which is the main conditioning feature of unions in some Western countries.

For managers, the system of regular annual pay increments based on seniority also means that they have little interest in profitability as such, since there is little chance for them to accumulate capital, and financial incentive schemes are rare. Only through his annual bonuses is a manager affected by the company's profitability. This is thought to be one reason why Japanese managers are more interested in size and growth than profits. Another reason is that the 'clan' system means that a manager's most honourable achievement is to increase his 'clan's' market share, rather as real clan barons of old were expected to fight to expand the clan's territory.

However, lifelong employment, strongly associated with payment and promotion based purely on seniority and length of service, is under attack from economic and other factors, which have already led to considerable modifications to the system. (1) The tendency to increase the retiring age from fifty-five to fifty-seven or more, as the average life span of Japanese increases, means a higher proportion of workers in the upper wage and salary brackets, so forcing up costs. (2) The growing shortage of young workers is pushing up starting wages, so pushing up the whole payment pyramid (because the age differentials must be maintained), even though there is, if anything, a surplus of older men. (3) Younger men are in any case getting impatient with the system, especially those with mobile skills, like motor assembly workers. (4) The growing number of graduates means that ability is increasingly recognised as a criterion of promotion, rather than pure seniority.

The pure seniority system persisted in at least some Japanese firms until the 1950s. But it has steadily been modified to take account of these factors. However, attempts at total change, by introducing the concept of job evaluation, failed totally. Job evaluation entails (*a*) a direct relationship between pay and the content of the job being done; (*b*) evaluation of individual effort. But the Japanese tradition is (*a*) pay related to the status and age of the person, rather than the job he is doing, and (*b*) evaluation of group effort. Job evaluation therefore became one of a number of Western management techniques which simply did not fit the Japanese scene.

Instead, for managers at least, Japanese companies have tended to adopt, in one form or another, the 'ranking system', in which a man is assigned a 'rank'. In such a system, a man's rank tells you his personal status rather than the actual work he is doing. So, in Japanese industry, to call a man an 'assistant manager' does not denote his job but his personal rank, with the status, pay, fringe benefits and respect that go with it. Incidentally, this system also gives rise to some bizarre titles, if literally translated—like 'Lord of the Shop' and 'Living Dictionary of the Office'.

The Japanese ranking system takes note of academic background, length of service, and ability. There is a close connection between rank and pay, but a loose connection between rank and job held. The system is certainly a compromise between the old and the new. But it has the advantage that it mitigates the strict hierarchy based on seniority, by enabling a good man to be moved up quicker, perhaps being given the power without, at first, the rank (because of the loose connection between rank and job held). At the same time the system consoles the less good man with a higher rank while leaving him in a less responsible position.

A few examples will show how this works. According to a survey conducted by the Japan Management Association, the Toyo Rayon company has thirty ranks, the new recruit being assigned to one of the three lowest. Speed of promotion depends on performance, *but* there is a *maximum* number of years for which a man stays in each rank, so that the man with the worst performance is promoted only at the end of that maximum period; i.e. this introduces the pure seniority and service element. But the best man gets on twice as fast as the worst man. A further feature is interesting. The divisions of the company can hire and fire non-graduates, but not graduates. But the company has a special exam which, if passed, enables a non-graduate employee to be treated as if he were a graduate. In another big company, the middle and senior management is graded into one of four ranks, and promotion from one rank to the next depends on years of service, salary level reached, and ability. But promotion to a higher job depends on having *previously* reached the rank appropriate to that higher job.

At Toyota, despite its air of a more 'Western' company, there are minimum periods of service for qualifying for certain ranks. For section chief, that minimum period is fifteen years. For assistant manager (the next highest grade), another five years is needed, and for manager, another two years. Then, from the ranks of the managers, the board of directors (who are all working directors) are selected. For blue-collar workers, similar rules apply. For example, a blue-collar man needs twenty years' service to qualify for consideration for

what the computer is all about. This rule includes existing managers, right up to the top level. However, Mitsubishi admits that it has yet to develop any systematic use of training courses related to a skill inventory of the company, as might be found in a progressive Western company.

Promotion for the new managers is determined by a combination of ability, age, and year of graduation from university. At the beginning, says the company, there is a special feeling between graduates of the same year, and so their promotion must be similar. But after several years, ability becomes more influential, within certain limits (those limits are gradually loosening, but will not disappear, the company maintains). Similarly, salary increases used to be a straightline progression with age, but this is also being modified. For one thing, the growing shortage of young recruits is driving up starting salaries, relative to salaries paid later in a manager's career (possibly no bad thing, given the low level of such starting salaries until recently). A manager's annual bonuses are determined by his superior in relation to his age, to his salary, and to the company's profitability. An average annual bonus total for a manager might be 22 per cent of his salary, and that looking only at basic salary a man of fifty might be earning about six times his starting salary with the firm.

One other feature of MHI also typifies an important aspect of Japanese industry—the system of quality control, which centres essentially, not on inspectors, but on the workers themselves. In almost all Mitsubishi plants, workers in each section meet together in their free time, possibly under the chairmanship of the foreman, and at the foreman's house, to discuss the way the job is done, and how to do it better. Once, this was done entirely without pay for the four to six hours a month that these discussions might take up. Now, Mitsubishi pays a token two hours' pay per month in recognition of these efforts—which are in turn very valuable to the company. This practice again derives from the social/family relationship which exists in a big Japanese company, and is another of its benefits.

This type of group quality control is frequent in Japanese industry, and is closely parallel in spirit to another movement—the so-called Management Self-Development programme, or MSD. This is run by the Japan Management Association, among others. In a typical case, groups of ten or so managers of the same rank get together once a month for study sessions, out of working hours. They are supplied with study material by the JMA, and their company often provides a classroom for them to use, and visiting speakers. The participants choose their own areas of study. This is seen as a superior substitute for the system of sending managers on courses decided for them by the personnel department, since it leaves the basic initiative with the individual manager. Also, like the quality control sessions among the workers, these study sessions throw up ideas and suggestions for improvements in company operations.

2. MATSUSHITA ELECTRIC INDUSTRIAL. One of the most remarkable companies in Japan, if not in the world, is Matsushita Electric Industrial. Its blend of lofty social idealism and ruthless pursuit of profit is difficult for Western minds to accept at face value. Matsushita is in fact the most profitable of all Japanese companies, in absolute value of earnings. In terms of sales, it is the second largest Japanese electrical manufacturer, according to *Fortune's* 1968 rankings, and the fourth largest Japanese manufacturer of any kind.

But Matsushita achieves these sales and profit results on an asset base which is about half that of the three biggest companies (Hitachi, Mitsubishi Heavy Industries, Yawata Iron and Steel). Over the last ten years, net income as a proportion of sales has been steadily pushed up from 4·7 per cent to 6·3 per cent, and over the last three years, since the current Japanese consumer boom set in, the annual sales increase has been of the order of 25–35 per cent. Sales last year, not including associate companies of various kinds, were about £550 m. As a result, Matsushita is a blue chip on Japanese stock exchanges, and a favourite among foreign investors (who hold over 10 per cent of its shares).

But at the same time, Matsushita managers will deny that profit is their motive. 'Service, not profit, is the objective', a senior executive said. 'Profit is not what we can earn—it is given to Matsushita by society in appreciation for its services.' A Matsushita director explained the company's profit concept in similar terms. 'If a company fails to make its profit, it has committed a social blunder or sin, according to our philosophy. The society to which Matsushita belongs entrusts it with capital and manpower for Matsushita to get results. Profit is the appreciation of society, the reward to Matsushita for what it has done.' What is more, a large chunk of that reward goes back to society, because Matsushita is naturally the largest taxpayer in Japan.

Every morning, before work begins, all employees stand at their work place and sing in chorus the company song, also a statement of belief, and ending with the words: 'Grow, industry, grow, grow, grow! Harmony and sincerity! Matsushita Electric!'

The company, also has a written statement of beliefs, to which employees must subscribe. It begins with a 'general principle', which is: 'To recognise our responsibilities as industrialists, to foster progress and to promote the general welfare of all: and to devote ourselves to the further development of the world's culture.' There follows a 'general creed', which runs: 'Progress and development can be realised only through the unity and cooperation of each member of the company. For this reason, each of us must keep this idea constantly in mind as we devote ourselves to the welfare of the company.' The third section is a list of seven articles of faith: National pride through industry:

Open-mindedness: Cooperation: Achievement: Common courtesy: Coordination: Gratitude.

In addition to this basic statement of philosophy, the company adopts a set of slogans for each year. In 1968, for instance, the slogans were: (1) Let's work together to make Matsushita Electric one of the best companies in the world. (2) Let's double our productivity through creative thinking and original ideas. (3) Let's develop new and original products using our own techniques and engineering resources. In 1969, the slogans changed to: (1) Understand the spirit with which the company began, and apply it now. (2) Creative thinking and application to give research and development results of a world standard. (3) In love and spirit of harmony, let us make our working place an ideal place of work.

To Western ears, all this may sound like a lot of verbal paraphernalia, reminiscent of the worst sort of Victorian paternalist industrialists, who insisted on ramming moral codes down the throats of their workers. Also, one must make allowances for the difficulty of translating the naturally rather flowery Japanese method of expression. But no one who has seen Japanese teamwork and understood the strong spirit of group loyalty that is characteristic of the Japanese and of Matsushita, will underrate the effect that these company slogans and principles have on employees at all levels (managers also sing the company song at the end of committee meetings).

Probably, the Matsushita principles are no more than a particularly explicit and extreme version of what many Japanese employees and managers feel and think. What needs explaining is how Matsushita manages to combine these unusually explicit ideals with such unusually high profits. The Victorian manufacturers who did the same in Britain are regarded with some cynicism. It is assumed that their moralising was just a more or less fraudulent cover for the money-making. But it would be rash to make that assumption with the Japanese (and, just possibly, with the Victorians as well).

Not surprisingly, Matsushita's philosophy also extends to the actual products it turns out. According to the same director, Masaji Hino, this part is called 'the watertap philosophy'. In précis form, his account of it goes something like this: 'Imagine a heavily burdened horse led up a hill by a man who finds a watertap half-way up, and stops and gives the horse a drink. The horse then gets to the top of the hill. The simile means that domestic appliances must be abundant like water, to make life easier for people. To implement this philosophy, it means low-cost, high-quality products, with good service. Quality means research and development, to get good products compared to our competitors. Low cost means increased productivity by everyone, the ideal being that the cost should be as low as that of the water from the tap (i.e. nothing). Service means that goods should be easy to use and provided with full instructions.'

Matsushita's philosphy derives from a very unusual man—seventy-five-year-old Konosuke Matsushita, the company founder (fifty years ago) and its current chairman. Matsushita, whose present 5 per cent shareholding in the company makes him a multi-millionaire, not to say Japan's largest private taxpayer, began work at eleven years of age in Osaka as an apprentice to a maker of charcoal braziers. That was in 1905. In 1917 he set up his own business in one room, making two-way electric lamp sockets, on a capital of 200 Japanese yen (a tiny sum, equivalent to the sales value of about 200 of his sockets). Matsushita's story after that is one of hard bargaining, fine costing, calculated risks and sheer entrepreneurship. He is regarded in Japan as a typical product of the merchant tradition of Osaka.

After the war he was 'purged' by the Allied administration because he had contributed to the Japanese war effort. But he was later 'depurged', partly as a result of petitions from his employees. His interest in the moral welfare of his employees and of Japan in general developed at the same period. In 1946 he coined his now famous slogan, 'Peace and Happiness through Prosperity', or PHP for short—a movement which now has its own Institute and its own journal, selling not far off a million copies each issue. A Japanese biography of Matsushita says that 'in contrast to the uplift in daily living standards, Matsushita found that the ethical standards of the people did not improve likewise . . . the PHP movement accordingly began to place stress on cultural and spiritual factors'. As a result, Matsushita is almost as famous in Japan for PHP as he is for his radios (marketed under the 'National' label and, in the US, under the 'Panasonic' name). 'Matsushita's main interest', says Hino, 'is to educate his employees— people first, products second'.

But the enigma is that *pari passu* with his growing interest in moral matters, Matsushita has developed one of the tightest management control systems to be found in any company in the world. Interestingly, this was also in origin an import from abroad—from Philips of Holland, to be exact. Japanese are familiar with the idea of borrowing product and technical know-how from abroad, and are perfectly familiar with the gamut of US management techniques. But when, in the early 1950s, Matsushita began installing a complete management system from abroad, there were many doubters. It would just not work in Japan. The joint venture company which Matsushita began in Japan with Philips at about the same period (Matsushita Electronics, in which Philips has a 35 per cent stake) was more acceptable, because more conventional. But the Japanese company is above all a social organisation, resistant to alien traditions, and importing a complete management system meant, in effect, a social upheaval. But Konosuke Matsushita insisted on having the whole Philips system installed, and since then it has been developed and polished to a degree that Philips might envy. Matsushita Electric is, like most Japanese industrial organisations, really a group of companies with varying financial and management relationships between themselves. At the periphery, there are about 400 sales companies for various of Matsushita's 3,000 different products (in all of which Matsushita has at least a 51 per cent stake), plus nineteen sales or manufacturing companies overseas. Then there are forty-seven 'associated' companies, eleven of which are quoted on the stock market. These companies are of two kinds. Some make and sell their own products, even in competition with Matsushita. Others supply Matsushita with components, and in these companies again Matsushita has at least a 51 per cent stake. In addition, Matsushita Electric itself is split into forty-nine divisions, and each of these forty-nine is treated as if it were a separate company—that is, as a separate profit centre. The total number of profit centres in the organisation is said to be about 130. The basic principles on which they are all run are the same as those applying to the divisions of Matsushita Electric itself.

The divisions have no less than four business plans, running concurrently. One, the most detailed, is semi-annual. Then there is an annual plan: a three-year plan: and a long-term plan. The plans, particularly the semi-annual ones, are submitted to Hino for detailed scrutiny. They cover production, sales, income, expenditure, investment and personnel. Hino says that he usually trims these plans slightly to make them 'more conservative', and they then go to Mr Matsushita for final approval. Subsequent monthly reports from the profit centres are analysed by Hino's staff at headquarters, and he himself sees the 'yellow signal' cases, where there are signs of deviation from the targets. The results of the HQ analysis are fed back to the divisions, together with advice. Hino and his staff also visit the divisions frequently, to reinforce their advice. It is said that the reporting system is in fact even stricter than this would suggest. Each division is said to telephone in its results at the end of *every day,* so that these results can be collated and put on Mr Matsushita's desk by the time he comes in the next morning.

The company also likes to emphasise its 'conservatism' in financial matters, and describes it as an antidote to the overoptimism which the company's rate of expansion could inspire. But it is a conservatism which is also a method of control. For Matsushita, uniquely for a Japanese company, sticks largely to a policy of financing expansion from retained earnings, and this enabled it to weather the last recession in Japan better than most. Matsushita not only cuts bank borrowing to a minimum, it also avoids lending out money from the centre to the divisions. If a division asks for money, its finances are closely scrutinised to find out whether it ought to be able to find the money itself. If head office does then lend, it lends at an interest rate higher than that prevailing at the banks. But recently, no such intra-company loans have in fact been made.

For basically, Matsushita men explain, loans of this type contravene another article of company philosophy —that concerning fair competition. It would be unfair to use the profits of one division to help the competitive position of another division. For example, Matsushita's radio division must compete fairly and independently with other radio manufacturers, as if it were a separate company. Similarly, there is no question of taking a lower profit margin on exports. About 20 per cent of production goes abroad, but the return is the same as on home sales. (Fair competition it may be, but it is also good business: Matsushita simply will not carry a product that does not yield sufficient profit—it dropped computers as soon as their problems became apparent.)

In accordance with this philosophy, each division is allocated a 'working fund' and a fixed investment of a determined value, together called its 'internal capital', and then the division is expected to get on with it, without further financial help from HQ. What is more, the company follows a strict policy of settling bills in cash at the end of every month, so that divisions cannot finance themselves by withholding payments to creditors.

Each division has to produce a profit margin, out of which it contributes to HQ for tax and dividends. It then pays for new investment, and the surplus still left is deposited with HQ, which redeposits it with various banks. Such is the profitability of Matsushita that its divisions have not only financed most of their growth from retained earnings, but have also in this way created bank deposits which easily exceed in value such long-term loans and debentures as the company has.

Although Konosuke Matsushita is now an old man, his son-in-law and adopted son, Masaharu Matsushita, is the president of the company. At fifty, he will presumably run the company for some while to come, on much the same lines as Konosuke. But it is hard to believe that the totally idiosyncratic nature of Matsushita Electric will survive its founder, since the firm, in all its aspects, is very much his own personal creation.

These examples show how Japanese firms have created a synthesis between the old and the new, each in its own way. But this adjustment of old to new is bound to be a continuing process, and it may be that the real tests of the worth of the Japanese system, as so far evolved, have yet to come. For one thing, the decade of growing consumer affluence in Japan has certainly presented opportunities to management: but it is adversity which really shows up the resilience of management, and it will be interesting to see what happens when a significant recession sets in—as, sooner or later, it must.

Secondly, the growing shortage of labour is creating employment problems, and may lead to pressure to revise the system, and may also lead to trade unions making greater use of the bargaining strength that a labour shortage will give them. Thirdly, and perhaps most important, Japan has until recently been a heavily protected market, with foreign direct investment very circumscribed, and largely concentrated in oil. By about 1972, these limitations must be removed, except for certain key areas like computers. Then Japanese managements will be confronted on their home ground with a direct challenge from foreign, and particularly American, managements. This will perhaps force further approximation to Western methods—and finally show how good Japanese managers really are.

JAPAN
business and
industrial
sectors

*Efficiency and teamwork: key factors in
Japan's economic success.*

8

Service Industries

Trading companies

Mitsui Bussan, whose sales aggregated 6,000 m dollars (£2,470 m) in fiscal 1968, is at the centre of a project for all the thirty-four Mitsui enterprises to build a twenty-four-storey skyscraper computer complex outside Tokyo to provide an information syndicate and nerve centre for the entire Mitsui family. Mitsubishi Shoji, whose 1968 sales were even higher, is involved in a similar plan to streamline communications and pool data between itself and its twenty-four sister enterprises spanning, as in Mitsui's case, the full range of manufacturing industry, banking and commerce.

These two projects provide a graphic illustration of the new kind of initiative being taken by Japan's trading houses to keep on top. They originated after World War I as agencies for Japanese industry to secure the foreign raw materials it needed and the export outlets for its products. They still perform this function.

Mitsubishi Shoji, for instance, announced, in 1969, a joint venture with an Indonesian firm for lumber development in Kalimantan, and Sumitomo Shoji was given the task of organising uranium supplies for the consortium of Sumitomo companies which is going into the nuclear power industry in a big way. One or other of the big Japanese trading houses is up to the hilt in Congo copper, in most of the undersea oil exploration ventures in South-east Asia and in the big mining schemes of Latin and North-west America.

They are also geared to secure export orders for Japanese products, acting as exclusive agents for their sister-firms at home in the manufacturing business and also for smaller independent producers unable to carry out their own export diplomacy. Mitsubishi Shoji, for example, has signed a contract for the supply of a 3.12 m dollar (£1.3 m) satellite communication station at Kuantan in Malaysia. Not that the trading houses are always the best export agent to have: Matsushita radios, Honda motorcycles, Canon cameras and Toyota cars have all done very well indeed without utilising their services.

Indeed, the search for profitable international trading has led the ex-*zaibatsu* firms into novel paths. They now organise consortia of Japanese firms to tender for such large contracts as the Lam Dom Noi dam in Thailand (won by Toyomenka, Mitsui and Sumitomo interests) or the 55 m dollar (£23 m) Iranian cold-rolled steel sheet project in which Mitsubishi Shoji, Mitsui Bussan, Toyomenka and Marubeni-Iida all collaborated.

Technical consultancy services are offered in order to bait potential customers in this class, and they are being revamped in anticipation of the many civilian rehabilitation and development projects which a settlement in Vietnam is likely to throw up in South-east Asia.

Combination deals—which amount to swapping a ship for oil of the same value, or equipment for produce —are increasingly frequent. Triangular commerce is also exploited where it is feasible: a trading firm will sell machinery to India and help the customer to find the foreign exchange to pay for it by selling Indian products in new markets. Mitsui Bussan has helped Indonesia find the overseas credits with which to buy Canadian wheat.

The Soviet and East European markets lend themselves to these complicated arrangements. Mitsubishi Shoji sold the Romanians a dry cell battery in exchange for marble. In some cases the Japanese act as a channel of technology between two foreign countries, as in the sale to the Soviet Union (through Mitsui Bussan) of a 48 m dollar (£20 m) ethylene plant made in Japan but using American techniques and paying royalties to the United States.

The trading firms also assist Japanese manufacturers to set up subsidiary operations overseas, including the location of suitable local equity partners. Mitsui Bussan and Mitsui Petrochemical were setting up a new subsidiary in 1969 in the United States, which will in turn form a joint venture with American interests to make petrochemical products—a challenge to the behemoth which would have seemed unthinkable a decade ago.

Marubeni-Iida has acquired a Belgian car sales company as an entry into the EEC market, and in 1969 the Mitsui group was planning to build in Antwerp a processing and distribution centre for its products in the EEC. The group's trading firm, Mitsui Bussan, inevitably takes the lead in this kind of development.

But now there is a tendency to set up manufacturing plant in low-wage neighbouring countries, especially South Korea, Taiwan, Hong Kong, the Philippines and Thailand, to cater for the Japanese market. Shirts and simple electronic items are the favourite commodities for this kind of exercise, which is likely to assume greater proportions in the future.

When all is said and done, however, the trading houses depend on the home market for their bread and butter. They handle 60 per cent of Japan's exports, but 65 per cent of imports—and they distribute Japanese goods within Japan as well.

They have gone full tilt into the supermarket business. Mitsui Bussan has concluded arrangements with twenty large supermarket chains in Japan, providing them with the funds for construction of buildings in which its own group's equipment will be installed and their products (along with imported goods for which Mitsui holds the agency) will be sold on mass scale. Mitsubishi Shoji has inaugurated, in collaboration with American interests, a Gold Bond Stamp scheme which might also accelerate its own sales lines.

The leasing business is providing opportunities, too, for the trading firms—with cranes, heavy equipment and aircraft among the articles hired out to customers shy of buying outright. Housing, an industry about to boom in Japan as the Government comes to terms with the social unrest and political discontent generated by poor living environment for the urban Japanese, is a recent target for their attention.

Many of the trading houses now help put up new housing estates or blocks as an outlet for prefabricated parts, fixtures, fittings and furnishings from their own lists. Even C. Itoh and Marubeni-Iida have joined this bandwagon.

To the insular Japanese manufacturer the outside world seems an unfamiliar and hostile jungle best avoided unless you are absolutely sure of a killing. The Mitsubishi Shoji and Mitsui Bussan men, who are found throughout the nations of the world arranging any kind of business in which there is some small percentage for Japan, see the world for what it really is—a proliferating network of business relationships out of which no sane man would opt.

So the trading firms were the real force behind Japan's belated conversion from protectionism. Mitsui invested in the ICI fertiliser plant in New South Wales in spite of the fact that it would supplant a Japanese export, and Mitsubishi Shoji now holds agencies for the import of foreign cars in spite of its domestic loyalty to Mitsubishi Heavy Industries (the car maker, significantly, which broke ranks in 1969 to collaborate with Chrysler in assembling Plymouth Valiants in Japan).

The senior executives in Mitsui Bussan and Mitsubishi Shoji are giants in Japan, men who know their world and its pulse, and who prod their nervous compatriots firmly into the trials of an adult relationship with a world whose communication system is based on non-Japanese cultural values. They may prove to be the saviours of the Japan-Western relationship and, since that in turn is seen by some as the guinea-pig for the whole coloured–white relationship in tomorrow's universe, of the eventual North–South accommodation.

Not that they are superhuman or always rational. Britain's Rolls-Royce got into trouble not so long ago, landing a sale to one of the ex-*zaibatsu* companies when its own agent in Japan belonged to a rival group. Since the after-sales servicing would have had to be done by the rival Japanese engineers of the other group, the customer finally refused to go through with the deal. But that was unusual: in the normal event patriotism keeps the trading houses in step.

Top eight Japanese companies (parents only)

| COMPANY | FISCAL YEAR 1968 | |
| | TURNOVER | ASSETS |
	(million yen)	
Mitsubishi Heavy Industries	627,325	1,000,697
Toyota Motor	617,417	325,120
Nissan Motor	556,133	524,350
Hitachi	543,216	641,745
Matsushita Electric Industrial	531,749	368,289
Yawata Iron and Steel	469,330	807,389
Toshiba	433,090	516,845
Fuji Iron and Steel	411,138	580,804

Source: Nomura Securities.

9

The banks

In the second half of 1969 use of newly installed, highly sophisticated electronic computer systems by the Japanese in handling financial transactions between banks had begun to speed progress towards reorganisation of the nation's banking institutions. Computers have proved their worth in permitting efficient and swift transmission of hourly data at a time when Japan's miracle economy is apparently in continuous upswing.

Pressure for mergers and reform in the banking world has come from Finance Ministry officials who are losing patience with conflicts of interest among various types of banks that have delayed wholesale revisions in the field. The Financial System Research Council, an advisory body to the Finance Ministry, sees the new technological developments in computer data processing and transmission already racing ahead of policy planners through creation of working ties—probably leading to joint operations and perhaps consolidations. The major problem now being resolved is heavy telephone line charges involved in use of computer systems between institutions.

Many of the larger city banks have started installing direct 'on-line' computer communications systems connecting main offices with all branches. When the new computer systems are completed, Japanese banks will have a closely integrated financial system. Completion is expected before 1972. Importance of the computer programmes being noted, some of Japan's most prominent bankers are having second thoughts, however. Sumitomo bank president Shozo Hotta fears that confidential information may leak through the computer system. Fuji bank president Yoshizane Iwasa thinks the programmes may work so well that mergers will be considered unnecessary. Yet these worries are in the minority.

If, in spite of the thinking of bankers Hotta and Iwasa, the most likely outcome is for the financial institutions to be encouraged to reorganise the major banks and smaller financial institutions into several large groups, it may develop eventually into a 'national system' suggested by the Japanese Bankers' Federation: computer-operated programmes connecting all banks which would permit depositors to do business through any financial institution throughout the country. This concept has frightened Japan's small financial organisations, now in process of seeking mergers or amalgamations, into speeding up reorganisation plans.

Under prompting from the Finance Ministry and the Bank of Japan, the Financial System Research Council has been discussing creation of a new system of medium-term deposits, transferable certificates of time deposits, establishment of a deposit insurance system and handling of trust business by commercial banks. The long-term credit banks and the banking institutions engaged in trust business, for example, are strongly opposed to the plan to create the system of three- or two-year time deposits. They fear, with good cause, that such a system would enable other banking institutions to encroach upon their operations.

The truth is that not a few members of the Council have announced they are inclined towards maintenance of the present financial system despite a long list of malpractices and weak points exposed over the past decade. Why have a considerable number of Council members lost the enthusiasm for reorganisation shown when they started studying the problems of the system in the autumn of 1967? After all, bankers had been dominated by the view that reorganisation was absolutely necessary to meet an anticipated slowing down of Japan's economic growth in the 1970s. It is simply that their present confidence in a continuing boom is sufficient to remove any sense of crisis.

The aim, then, of the Finance Ministry and the Central Bank to reform the specialised structure of the financial system may have to be abandoned if opposition gains much more strength. Yet statements by powerful Bank of Japan authorities indicate that the main battle may not have been joined. Japan's big city banks want the Central Bank to remove official controls over deposit rates, lift restrictions on banking functions to permit them to diversify their services and to allow them to issue certificates of deposits. City banks also want to be allowed to engage in trust business, a field now allocated almost exclusively to the trust banks allied with the city banks, the mutual banks seek to be permitted to move into the medium and long-term credit field. These targets are blocked by the other financial institutions.

By giving in on some of these points, the Central Bank could possibly obtain valuable supporters for the Government's more drastic reorganisation plans. But obviously the sweeping revisions desired in the system will have to be weighed against the bitter prospect of abandoning many of the financial controls so dearly cherished over the years by the Central Bank authorities.

10

The stock exchanges

Stock exchanges were established in Tokyo and Osaka in 1878, and these two centres still account for some 95 per cent of turnover, the balance being transacted on seven local exchanges.

A new Tokyo Stock Exchange was constructed in 1949, when securities legislation was passed on the United States pattern. The structure was modified early in 1968 so as to include, for the first time, trading in bonds as well as shares and to transfer from the banks to brokers all new issue business.

Members of the Exchange are companies and not individuals. As a result of more stringent screening procedures, their numbers were reduced in April 1968, to 277 from the 430 that were licensed in 1965. About three-quarters of business is done by four firms.

As part of a move to attract private investment, company accounting, particularly for quoted companies, has been tightened up, although disclosure of true earnings still falls short of American and British standards.

Some 6 million private investors were estimated at the end of 1968 to hold 43 per cent of listed shares. The extent of popular participation in the stock market is probably second only to the United States.

The government is able to restrict foreign holdings to

not more than 20 per cent (sometimes 25 per cent) of a company's share capital. Most shares have a par value of 50 yen and rights issues are normally made at par. The Stock Exchange is divided into two Sections, the First Section having more restrictive listing requirements than the Second, which is made up of smaller and more speculative issues.

Trading sessions take place from 09.00 hours to 11.00 hours and from 13.00 hours to 15.00 hours on weekdays. There is a morning session on Saturdays. There is no futures market on the Japanese stock exchanges. Overseas investors thinking of the possibility of investing in Japan can do so through the offices of the Japanese securities companies in such major cities as London, Paris, New York or Washington. Orders may be placed by mail, telegraph or telephone. Each order should include full information as to the name of the security, the price, number of shares and the duration of the order.

Because of the special documentation required for investments by non-residents and foreign nationals, particularly when foreign currency is involved, overseas investors can appoint one of the Japanese securities houses as a Standing Proxy. Under a proxy arrangement, the purchase and sale of securities can be expedited and collections and remittance of dividends and sales proceeds arranged.

Japanese securities houses charge a fee for such services. The charge is usually an annual 0.10 yen per share supervised for the account as of the end of September, with minimum and maximum charges of 2,000 yen (5.56 dollars or 56 shillings) and 100,000 yen (280 dollars or £110), respectively. After receiving stock certificates and notifying the buyer. Japanese securities companies will have the certificates registered to ensure that the dividends and new share rights are properly credited and paid.

As 1969 drew to a close, there were three separate sorts of problems of major significance in Japan's often volatile stock exchanges. There was the long-term 'insider information' question, the medium-term failure of the disenchanted general public to return to the market, and, the very short-term (it was hoped) disappearance of the big-money foreign investor. Finance Ministry authorities have a committee studying the matter of reforms which might be adopted to eliminate most of the more flagrant abuses of inside information. The chief target is executives of listed firms (and the securities houses handling their stocks) who often use privileged information to profit from market movements. Under consideration are regulations requiring fuller public disclosures, tightened controls on trading practices, and restrictions against 'privileged profits'.

Some officials in the Finance Ministry's Securities Bureau feel that insiders—not only company executives, but also executives of securities firms—should be barred from buying and selling shares on the basis of inside information. The securities houses strongly object to such a ban, pointing out that this kind of operation is fundamental to their business. Japan's securities firms are the major traders in the market, they contend. In essence, there would be no effective market without their participation, since the shares they trade for their own account often amount to something over half of total turnover.

More crippling to the reputation of the exchanges is the refusal of Japan's small investor to play a part in the market. After the dark days of January 1962, when the Dow Jones Index fell 571 points, the public was finally coming back into the market in mid-1968, a fairly good year. New record orders followed a domestic boom assisted by a strong trade and payments position and the Index climbed steadily toward 2,000 yen (5.56 dollars or 56s) in what looked like the first real bull market since 1961. Then the professionals, after the August-September rise, quickly unloaded and in less than a week the Index lost 150 yen (0.42 dollars or

3*s* 6*d*) to scare off the small investors.

Even when the Dow Jones Index entered a period of continuous growth in the spring of 1969, reaching an all-time record high of 2,029.59 yen (5.64 dollars or 47*s*) in June, the small-scale investor stayed out. His fears were seemingly justified when the Index suddenly nose-dived, losing 195.86 yen (0.56 dollars or 4*s* 8*d*) in one week, the second worst price loss in Japan's history. The rise had been too fast and sharp, according to the securities houses.

On the whole, however, the market subsequently became more solid, thanks to the various developments in 1968. Two agencies created to prop up the market in the bad days of 1964 and early 1965—the Japan Securities Holding Association and the Japan Joint Securities Company—were able to sell off most of their 400,000 m yen (1.1 m dollars or £450,000) in share holdings. They no longer hang over the exchange floors. Reforms pushed through by the Finance Ministry have weeded out the weaker securities houses, and the survivors are in better financial shape.

The short-term problem is that, thanks partly to rumoured changes in parity of major Western currencies and growing inflationary pressures in Europe and America, foreign investors began purchasing Japanese stocks in earnest in the first few months of 1968. Then in July of 1969 overseas orders fell off and selling began.

Foreign investors apparently attached more value to capital gains than to the yield in making purchases, and quickly retired their money when the world financial crisis seemed to be further off. Easing of Japanese Government restrictions on foreign holdings of local growth stocks and remittances of proceeds does not appear to have encouraged overseas buyers to stay in the market. As a result, the Bank of Japan considers the inflow of funds from foreign investors to be something in the order of hot money.

11

Tourism

Despite considerable promotional efforts in recent years, the tourist industry, according to dispassionate statistics, is a drain on Japan's balance of payments. In 1964, the first year that the average Japanese could obtain foreign currency for leisure trips abroad, nationals spent 78 m dollars (£32.5 m) abroad, and the country earned only 62 m dollars (£25.8 m) from foreign visitors. The deficit since has grown bigger every year.

The basic dollar allowance for spending abroad has been raised from 500 dollars to 700 dollars (£208 to £292) for each Japanese traveller, and this limit is likely to be relaxed. If Okinawa is regarded as a foreign destination—and the Japanese must spend dollars on that US-administered island—more than half a million Japanese made trips abroad in 1968. The Economic Planning Agency believes that the number of Japanese going overseas will exceed one million a year by 1975, and that they will spend 467.8 m dollars (£195 m). Japanese authorities estimate that 730,000 Japanese indulged the national bent for travel in 1969.

The influx of foreign visitors has increased much more slowly. Around 418,000 overseas visitors came to Japan in 1968, and even the most optimistic estimate puts the total at not much more than 600,000 in 1969. There is, however, the hope that EXPO '70 will boost foreign arrival figures to more than one million. Large numbers of South-east Asians, with their enormous interest in Japanese industrial accomplishments, will undoubtedly make the journey. There are wistful hopes that the more monied Europeans and Americans will arrive in quantity. The revised estimates for total attendance at EXPO '70 are that at least 40 million people, and possibly 50 million will be there. This means that on peak days attendance could be in the region of 500,000, a figure representing (apart from its foreign percentage) Japanese people from all over the islands heading for the new centre of leisure travel.

But even if, in this dawning era of jumbo jets, foreign visitors increase markedly in numbers, it would probably not reduce the year-to-year deficit dramatically. The relatively high cost of reaching Japan from Europe and the US, plus the high cost of living for foreigners, has caused travel agencies and package organisers to cut down increasingly on length of stay. Two or three days is now common, compared to more than a week in earlier patterns.

Charter flights and package tours, the meat and potatoes of the Japanese tourist industry, tend to whisk their charges off to Hong Kong and South-east Asia for better money value. It is true that in 1968 Japan reported a 42 per cent increase in tourist receipts to the OECD, but it is probable they spent only about 43 dollars daily. This sum would account for hotel, meals and transport, but would leave little over for a spending splurge. Entertainment for two in a typical Tokyo nightclub, for instance, would normally set the couple back by anything between 100 dollars and 200 dollars (£42–£84). Visitors are easily scared off by Japanese price tags, and tend to stick closely to their guided tour itinerary. During a bus tour of Osaka, which includes a bilingual guide, one can in the course of four hours visit three top carbarets for 11 dollars (£4 10s.), drinks excluded.

The country does, however, have an excellent system

of inexpensive inns and youth hostels, ideal for the hardy and adventurous who can tour as cheaply as in Europe by means of local public transport. The real barrier is language, especially in rural areas, and native foods are very much an acquired taste. These cheap living places, moreover, are usually jammed to the windowsills with Japan's own restless young people.

But there is a foreign tourist spin-off which blunts the hard impression given by the statistics. Westernised facilities developed to encourage foreign visitors have proved a great spur to the vast leisure industry which caters for tens of millions of nationals. Travel agencies handling domestic tours have grown in numbers from 2,392 in 1964 to 3,597 according to the latest estimate. Over half the country's adults spent at least two days at a holiday inn or hotel last year, spending on average 23.50 dollars (£10). Economic Planning Agency projections for the decade 1965 to 1975 say that by the end of the period domestic travel will have increased five-fold and annual spending would be in the region of 8.3 m dollars (£3.5 m). The Japanese tend to move in group tours, which is why even luxury Tokyo hotels reported an occupancy rate of more than 90 per cent throughout 1968.

Tokyo is estimated to have a shortage of 5,000 Western-style rooms but the Osaka area has added no less than 4,000 rooms to the 6,000 which it had before EXPO '70. When faced with an influx of 13,000 visitors for the 1969 Lions International convention, Tokyo was forced to find billets for the overflow in surrounding towns up to fifty miles away. There are at least ten major Western-style hotels at present under construction or planned, all of them with from 700 to 1,000 rooms, but there is some concern that this is still inadequate, especially if larger groups of people are to arrive on jumbo jets.

More than 400,000 foreign visitors were recorded in 1968, which included 138,657 businessmen. The overall total included 246,000 Americans, 25,480 Britons,

22,649 Australians, 13,272 Canadians and 12,046 Germans, while the rest were mainly Asians.

The Japanese exodus included more than 115,000 businessmen, mainly bound for the United States or Europe. The typical tourist tended to stick to South-east Asia. Japanese travel overseas, too, is tending to be at the level of cheaper package tours, and many young people take advantage of the cheaper sea and rail route through Siberia to Moscow and Europe.

12

The railways

Since the first super-express inaugurated the 320-mile Tokyo–Osaka service on 1 October, 1964, well over 200 million passengers have travelled on the New Tokaido Line, turning a potential white elephant into debt-burdened Japanese National Railway's biggest money-spinner. Income from the service has already covered the line's construction costs, and the service should show a clear profit within two years, when rolling stock and maintenance costs have been recouped. Earnings in 1969 on the line were around 840,000 dollars (£350,000) a day, and this looks set for a further boost in 1970 when JNR increases the length of the Hikari expresses—faster of the two services on the line, making the trip in three hours and ten minutes—from twelve to sixteen coaches, and steps up the number of trains running. Such expansion spells amazing confidence in these days of declining rail fortunes, but perhaps Japan had a head start over other countries in her decision to pioneer commercial high-speed rail services.

Prior to the New Tokaido Line's opening, the only practical way to travel between Tokyo and Osaka without taking a whole day to do so was by air—as the subsequent fall in domestic air travel bore out only too graphically for the airlines. There was of course a rail link between the two cities before 1964, and trains still run on this line; they take eleven hours and twenty-eight minutes to cover the distance. The new line also had the advantage of 'competing' with some of the worst roads of any advanced nation.

As recently as 1966, less than 10 per cent of Japan's roads were paved—only half of these asphalted—while a third of her roads were unsuitable for motor vehicles. All this is changing, as Japan faces up to the needs of the motor age with a succession of ambitious road-building programmes, designed to link all the country's major centres with national highways and expressways. Progress has been rapid, and motorists can now drive from Tokyo to Osaka via three new expressways, the latest of them—the 346·7-kilometre Tokyo–Nagoya Tomei Expressway—opened in 1969.

The country's rugged terrain makes construction of any major artery a formidable proposition—the Tomei Expressway passes over 271 bridges, 117 elevated sections and through 8·7 kilometres of tunnels—while the fragmentation of Japan into four main islands and countless smaller islands complicates the drawing up of any national plan. In view of this, and in the face of calls to wield an axe on unprofitable branch lines, it is a wonder that JNR is still thinking of expanding the rail network. But of course, rail chiefs can point to the success of the New Tokaido Line as proof of demand for high-speed rail services. The westward New Sanyo Line extension, from Osaka to Okayama, opens in 1972; a further extension to Hakata was officially approved in September 1969 and should be ready by 1975. Meanwhile JNR researchers optimistically push on with further development of high-speed trains and track.

The New Tokaido Line gives them quite a model to start from—a track of lengths of welded steel rail on rubber pads, set in concrete sleepers; automatic speed control through circuits laid in the track; track-side seismographs and anemometers to automatically cut off current from the 25-kV overhead wires in the event of a natural disaster, quite apart from such concessions to passenger comfort and service as radio telephones for the businessman who finds even three hours too long to be out of touch with the world whizzing by outside the double-glazed window.

Quite a contrast to the commuter trains which take the suburban Japanese to and from their work, with the famed student 'pushers' cramming luckless Tokyoites

One of the 100 mph Hikari expresses on the New Tokaido Line passes Kyoto, medieval capital of Japan.

into their overflowing carriages. But if the Japanese have their urban transport headaches these are soon forgotten when it comes to making the Grand Gesture. The Tokaido Line was a case in point, and so, too, is the decision to go ahead with construction of a 36·4-kilometre undersea tunnel to link the main island of Honshu with Hokkaido, to the north.

Test borings have been carried out since 1964, and Japan Railway Construction Corporation hopes to start full-scale construction in 1970; target date for completion is around 1975. It will be the longest tunnel in Japan—though shorter than the proposed Anglo-French Chunnel—with 32 kilometres of the total length under the sea.

At the other end of Honshu, debate centres on the choice of route for a giant suspension bridge across the busy sea lanes of the Inland Sea to join the island and its southern neighbour Shikoku. Debate has been flowing round the subject for a good few years now, and a final decision still seems out of sight. However, the Japanese did get around to spanning the 386 kilometres from Onomichi in Honshu to the Inland Sea island of Mukojima with a bridge 36·5 metres above the high-water mark, and this has been suggested as first stage in an island-hopping solution to the larger project.

Not much comfort maybe to the city dweller as he jams into his commuter train, but such far-reaching schemes and developments are rapidly obliterating memories of a pre-motor-age transport system in industrial Japan.

13

Capital and consumer goods

Steel

Since 1960 Japanese crude steel production has more than trebled from 22 million tons to 67 million tons— a phenomenon which must rank as one of the most remarkable records of expansion in the history of industrial development. And yet this industry retains the capacity to surprise even its leaders by its appetite for growth.

Every year since 1960, sound, hard-headed production forecasts have proved to be underestimates.

A buoyant export market, particularly in Europe and South America, has encouraged growth and continued demand on the home front has also played its part. Clearly the Japanese industry is an undisputed giant in the international steel world; it is third in line after the United States and the Soviet Union in production, and second to none in technical innovation. In 1968 the Japanese produced 67 million metric tons of crude steel, or 12·7 per cent of total world output. The United States produced 120·9 million tons and the Soviet Union some 106·2 million tons, according to the Japan Iron and Steel Federation. Despite its rapid expansion, Japanese production is likely to remain third in line in the early 1970s, but by the middle of the decade it should have the highest steel consumption *per capita* in the world.

Modern automated steel works on seaside locations are a major feature of the Japanese steel industry and the construction of huge new plants is going ahead rapidly. In 1969 there were some twenty-four steel works around the world with an annual capacity exceeding 4 million tons. Nine were in the US, eight were in Japan and six were in the Soviet Union. Of the ten largest blast furnaces in the world at last count, Japan had seven, the Soviet Union two and the Netherlands one. Much of Japan's technical success has been founded on foreign technology and know-how—which is often

One of the world's largest blast furnaces:
Sumitomo Metal Industries.

widely adopted in Japan ahead of the originating nation. But Japan has also developed its own techniques which are now being exported. It is evident that the swift diffusion of new technology through the Japanese steel industry has been a major contributing factor to its present success.

Peter Drysdale, an Australian economist who is a student of the Japanese steel industry, has summed up the six factors which have made the Japanese steel industry so internationally competitive in both price and quality. They were, he said, the efficient use of high quality raw materials; the favourable port-side location of new capacity; the swift import of new technology through an overwhelming proportion of new capacity; economies of scale in the production of basic iron and steel as well as milled products; relatively low wage costs, and automated production controls.

The industry has its problems, and two are particularly worrying to the leaders of the Japanese steel industry. One is the increasingly severe labour shortage, which however is not a direct threat to the industry with its increasingly automated plants. Indirectly it is the local steel consumers, particularly in the motor vehicle, shipbuilding and construction industries, who may have their growth stunted by the labour scarcity. The other major concern is the supply of raw materials. The industry in 1968 depended on foreign suppliers for more than 90 per cent of its iron ore and more than 70 per cent of the coking coal and these percentages will rise in the next five years. There is no great concern about the supply of iron ore—the vast reserves of the Pilbara region of Western Australia are comfortingly close and there are other big resources in South America and Africa. But coking coal is a different story. Prices are rising—in contrast to the price of iron ore from Australia (the major supplier), which is dropping. Coal resources are nothing like so abundant or convenient as iron ore, and to meet this problem, the industry has launched an ambitious programme covering Canada, South America,

Australia, Africa, Russia and Eastern Europe, to assess possible new sources.

Research is being conducted into methods of reducing coke ratios even further in the steel-making process and first steps have been taken to investigate the possibility of using cheaper nuclear fuel for firing blast furnaces. The Ministry of International Trade and Industry has expressed concern that the industry will enter a period in 1970 when expansion will threaten prices. It has been impossible to slow down the various capital expenditure programmes of the six major firms. In MITI's view, the supply–demand situation could be disturbed by over-investment in new plants and installation of highly technical equipment.

Top steel executives, on the other hand, see no reason to curtail programmes already well under way and scheduled to be completed in 1970 and 1971. Planning has been based, they point out, on steadily increasing demand both at home and abroad. Privately, they insist that the MITI bureaucrats have consistently been overly pessimistic in capacity forecasts. 'If we had listened to MITI,' a leading steel executive said, 'we would not have been ready to meet demand on the domestic and overseas markets and prices would have climbed much higher than they are now.' It is the rapid expansion of the industry, in the opinion of Japan's steelmen, which has built the base for much of this country's explosive economic growth over the last decade.

14

Shipbuilding

The Japanese shipbuilding industry, which boasts thirteen consecutive years of domination of world shipbuilding, feels that the European advantage of earlier delivery dates is no longer as great as it used to be. Although Japan has a backlog up to 1972/73, the Europeans have now also acquired a backlog nearly as great as this. Japan, therefore, is counting on modern techniques and experience, guaranteed delivery and lower prices, to give them an advantage.

On the problems side, the industry suffers from a lack of skilled workers, a higher wage bill, and rising prices of steel plate. Because of overtime and increasing costs, shipping firms have been warned that despite modernisation and rationalisation, prices of new vessels will go up.

On the labour question, Takao Nagata, President of Japan Shipbuilders' Association, said that labour accounts for between 25 and 30 per cent of the total costs of each ship, depending on its size, which is almost equal to that of some foreign yards with very efficient industries. Wages for the country's 200,000 employees have been rising at the rate of about 10 per cent a year. Despite this, more than 4,000 skilled workers quit each year during their employment term. The shipbuilders are attempting to handle the problem by expanded investment in labour-saving facilities, improved working conditions, and increased inducements for surpassing production quotas. Hitachi Shipbuilding and Engineering, for example, has been spending between 1,667 m and 1,944 m dollars (£695 m and £810 m) annually on new plant and equipment.

Japanese shipbuilders are not too concerned at the prospect of higher steel prices. They point out that the cost of ships in Europe has gone up as well since they depend on a large volume of imported steel. Confidence has been expressed that the Japanese rate of price increases may not be as steep as those in Europe. The Japanese have welcomed reports from Europe that steel prices in Britain went up by 10 per cent, which was reflected in the cost of ships to the extent of 3·5 per cent. It is felt that Japanese prices will not rise above 4 or 5 per cent, and the reflected increase in ship's costs will be not more than 1·5 per cent.

High hopes in the industry discount these problems, and give rise to predictions that new export orders in 1969 may be the largest, in tonnage terms, in history. The record year was 1966, when orders for 255 ships were received, totalling 8,742,756 tons. But these predictions are probably over-optimistic; it is in value and profits where the records might be set.

Despite previous indications that Japanese shipbuilders might be lagging behind Europe in the control of costs, the Ship Exporters' Association sees no difficulties until the mid-1970s. This view is not shared, however, by Nobuo Inouye, managing director of Hitachi Shipbuilding and Engineering, who sees the industry (now building half the world's new ships) suffering a partial recession after 1972 because of the labour shortage. Some observers believe that this threat could be removed by the Government's current domestic ocean-going merchant fleet programme, 1969–74, which may be expanded from its present target of 20·5 million gross tons to something near 26 million gross tons in the event of export orders falling off.

The launching of the Tokyo Maru *in 1966.*

In the meantime the Government provides considerable assistance in the matter of new export orders. In 1969, the Export-Import Bank of Japan set aside 461.9 m dollars (£192.4 m) for financing delivery of export vessels. For fiscal 1970 the figure is likely to top 484.5 m dollars (£202 m) if the Bank approves requests by members of the Shipbuilders Association.

There is, however, at least one top official in the Ministry of Transport who seems to feel that the merchant fleet expansion programme will not be the easy answer if a fall-off in export orders does occur. Mr Takeo Hori, Vice-Minister, has been trying to discourage any talk of expanding the six-year programme. He points out that there is doubt whether the nation's shipping interests want to increase their fleets proportionately. This may be the correct view, especially considering that shipowners have already lodged complaints to the effect that (compared with the Government's 24th Shipbuilding Programme for 1968) construction costs under the current programme are high, sometimes prohibitively so.

The Association admits that, already, the cost of building a 12,000-ton medium-speed cargo ship is 4·65 per cent higher than it was last year; a 100,000-ton combination ore and oil carrier is up 4·35 per cent. This is an indication of the price increases foreign shipping companies may expect over the next few years.

The Shipbuilders' Association fears that Japan's share of the world's new tonnage will drop to 45 per cent in 1973 from the 50 per cent enjoyed in 1968, mainly because construction costs are expected to rise by as much as 25 per cent during the next five years under pressure from climbing wage and material prices. Nevertheless, the Association predicted that actual tonnage launched by Japan during the period would increase as a result of world demand, rising from the 16·8 million gross tons of 1968 to approximately 24 million tons by 1973. 'Without considerable Japanese help, the world's yards naturally would not be able to meet requirements,' an association spokesman said. 'We'll most probably remain the world's leading shipbuilder despite our forthcoming trials.'

15

Motor cars

In 1949 Japan's motor industry produced 1,070 passenger cars, ten of which were exported. In 1959 car production was 78,598, domestic registrations totalled 73,271 and exports reached 4,884. In the first half of 1969, domestic registrations totalled 681,946 and five models topped the 50,000 figure (Toyota's Corona 118,960, Corolla 116,547; Nissan's Bluebird 87,459, Sunny 70,538; and Toyo Kogyo's Familia 52,247); in addition, 237,337 'light cars', of the 360-cc class, were registered. Passenger car production was averaging 200,000 monthly in 1969 and exports totalled 272,949 in the first half-year.

All the 1969 figures represent big increases on those for the corresponding point in 1968. At the half-year stage, Toyota, for instance, was 35 per cent ahead on 1968 in overall vehicle production, 50 per cent up on passenger car production, and 43 per cent ahead in passenger car exports. With these highly successful figures, there should be happy smiles on every motor manufacturer's face. But this is not so, for the past months have been clouded by a series of long-term anxieties and temporary near-panics, most of them deriving from the approach of capital liberalisation or the fact that Japan has now fully entered the age of motorisation.

Attitudes within the motor industry to capital liberalisation have been highly volatile over the past year. First there were confident predictions that 'We can be ready by 1970 or 1971, and by then we can have the industry so securely packaged in the Nissan and Toyota groups (and perhaps one other, comprising Mitsubishi Heavy Industries, Isuzu and Toyo Kogyo) that there will be no worthwhile remnant for any foreign motor-maker to infiltrate.' Then came proposals that liberalisation day be deferred and hints that Government (Ministry of International Trade and Industry, MITI) was dragging a reluctant and insufficiently prepared industry too precipitately into capital liberalisation; next, increased anxiety in some quarters when Ford announced an arrangement with Toyo Kogyo and Nissan for the joint production of automatic transmissions and, finally, near-panic when Chrysler proposed a partnership with Isuzu. This latter violates the understanding that a foreign company should not be permitted to associate with any existing Japanese motor manufacturer—in other words, let it saddle itself with a parts maker or a new company and leave it to fight to build up from such a weak bridgehead.

The Chrysler-Isuzu proposal also created ill-will and accusations of bad faith among the domestic makers, where talks had been going on quietly for some time on some form of association between Isuzu and Mitsubishi HI which might, in the outcome, have incorporated others of the hitherto unaligned producers. Some of the doubts have been allayed by an authoritative statement from the Vice-Minister of MITI to the effect that capital liberalisation is not to be advanced earlier than the beginning of fiscal 1972–73. But MITI has been known to change its mind before, and has tended to waver over matters concerning the motor industry.

There have been difficulties also for domestic sales forecasters, even in Toyota, which usually reads the market with great accuracy. Towards the end of 1968, Toyota's experts were suggesting that the Japanese consumer might be starting to lose enthusiasm for the private car as the most attractive of a long list of status symbols, and it was feared that saturation point might be much nearer at hand than the mid-1970s as had been earlier calculated. There had been a continuous and increasing boom for the 'people's car' since the introduction of a wide range of 1,000–1,100 cc models in 1966 and by 1968 this class, with 516,670, accounted for exactly one-third of domestic passenger car registrations (compared with 2·4 per cent in 1960 and 20 per cent in 1965).

But the faltering in the boom was shortlived and by late spring of 1969, faced, as all employers, with an acute and growing labour shortage, Toyota, for instance, was pointing ruefully to the gap between, on the one hand, production figures and, on the other, the sum of domestic registrations and export totals. To bridge this gap, Toyota planned to increase monthly production of all vehicles to 140,000 from the average 120,000 monthly figure for the first half of 1969; production of the 1,100 cc Corolla, now Toyota's best-selling model, was scheduled—perhaps too hopefully—for a monthly 50,000 before the end of 1969, in place of the monthly 32,000 at the end of the first half.

Then there has been the affair of the recall of defectives—up to one million vehicles brought in by Nissan and Toyota alone. Certainly, quality control, though much talked of, leaves much to be desired, the major culprits being the four million so-called 'medium and small enterprises', often woefully undercapitalised and employing a mere handful of workmen. Japan's strict and extensive officially controlled export inspection system exposes, yet does little to remedy, a regular export reject rate of up to 25 or 30 per cent in some products, such as electrical consumer goods, where, as with the motor industry, parts come mainly from this 'medium and small enterprise' sector where it is difficult for the assembler to maintain full control of quality.

It seems that for the moment at least little will blunt

the desire of the Japanese to become car owners. The national *per capita* income figure creeps towards the price of the 'popular' models, and there is a growing list of superficial attractions for the motorist—Tokyo has an ever-growing urban expressway system, Osaka has one for EXPO '70, and the opening of the Tokyo-Nagoya section in May of 1969 now affords a motorway linking the most heavily populated and highly produc-

Assembling the Datsun 2000 sportscar.

tive urban zones along the Pacific coastline from Tokyo to Kobe.

But such 'spectaculars' achieve little in easing the increasing traffic congestion in all the larger cities. On the main highways leading into Tokyo from the outer suburbs and satellite towns there are daily traffic jams, and Tokyo's air never seems free of the peculiarly heavy and bitter fumes that come from Japanese exhausts. It could well be, with the increasing recognition of the low standard of Japan's social stocks and with traffic congestion as the major grievance according to a public opinion poll conducted in 1969 by the Prime Minister's Office, that popular opinion might force planning for the improvement of conventional—rather than spectacular and toll-bearing—urban, suburban and interurban highways and that the private driver in Japan will at long last be given something of a square deal.

The steady buoyancy of the domestic market, as ever, acts as a solid base for increasing exports. Both Nissan and Toyota (which account for 80 per cent of exports) now transport to America in a fleet of custom-built, cost-cutting carriers from newly equipped exclusive wharves in Yokohama and Nagoya respectively. Expansion of exports to Europe (particularly to EEC member countries and Britain, where performance was poor) goes to plan, in line with deliberately unspectacular targets laid down by both Toyota and Nissan two years ago.

There are interesting developments in the South-east Asian area. With its association with Shinjin, the major motor manufacturer in South Korea, Toyota is well in the lead, in both production volume and price levels, from Ford and Fiat which have made similar arrangements with local producers. These are expected to meet domestic demand by 1971 and soon after the Korean government, apparently with the tacit agreement of Shinjin-Toyota, plans to join the ranks of exporters in the region.

If domestic demand in Japan, the export boom and

the critical labour shortage persist at present levels, it would be no small relief to Toyota (and perhaps other Japanese manufacturers will follow Toyota's lead elsewhere in the region) to off-load some of the burden of production and exports to the area to partners within the region.

16

Nuclear energy

A quarter-century after the devastation of Hiroshima and Nagasaki by the only atomic bombs dropped in anger, 'nuclear' remains a dirty word in Japan. A survey by the Japanese Prime Minister's office indicates that 63 per cent of the Japanese public still react negatively to mere mention of the word. It is this public attitude that, in part, has slowed the development of nuclear power generation in Japan. Construction programmes of Japan's nine regional electrical utilities have been consistently bogged down by difficulties in site acquisition. Fishermen, fearing contamination of their fishing waters, and villagers fearing some catastrophic accident, regularly and vociferously protest against attempts to instal nuclear power stations in their areas.

In 1969 there was only one nuclear power station in Japan generating atomic power on a commercial basis. This is a 166,000 kW station operated by the Japan Atomic Power Company, a consortium of the nine privately-owned regional electrical utilities and a multitude of equipment makers. But during the past sixteen years Japan has spent nearly 720 m dollars (£300 m) in preparing for a full-scale plunge into peaceful applications of atomic energy. With the help of massive public relations campaigns, sites have been acquired in remote coastal zones and construction has proceeded. Now Japan is about to emerge full-blown into the age of atomic power generation.

At the end of 1969, there were five commercial-scale nuclear power plants under construction in Japan, aggregating 2,381 MW in capacity, two more totalling 1,176 MW scheduled to get under way within the next six months, and two others, with a combined capacity of 1,284 MW set to break ground next year. In all, Japanese utilities have firm plans to be operating thirteen nuclear power stations by the end of 1975, generating 7,257 MW of electricity, and plans for a total of thirty-two operating nuclear plants by the end of 1980. By 1985 Japanese nuclear stations will have a capacity of 53,700 MW, supplying an estimated 30 per cent of Japan's entire electric power needs.

Britain played a major role in getting Japan launched on the nuclear trail. The only currently operating commercial atomic power reactor in Japan is the advanced Calder Hall-type gas-cooled unit built by the General Electric Company and installed at the JAPCO site in cooperation with the United Kingdom Atomic Energy Authority. A second JAPCO reactor, which was due to start up in December, 1969, is a 357 MW boiling water reactor being built by General Electric of the United States. The two plants being built for Japan's largest regional utility, Tokyo Electric Power Company, are also GE BWR's, and Tokyo Electric has selected the same type of reactor for construction of its third station, which will get under way in 1970.

Kansai Electric Power Company, which serves the Osaka area, selected the Westinghouse pressurised-water reactor for its first three atomic stations. Chubu Electric Power Company is considered likely to go with the GE BWR and most of the other Japanese utilities appear to be leaning the same way. To be sure, GE and Westinghouse have done an aggressive selling job in Japan. GE has entered into technical and manufacturing agreements with such top-flight and influential Japanese industrial enterprises as Tokyo Shibaura Electric Company and Hitachi, Westinghouse has developed its long-standing ties with the powerful Mitsubishi group. The American companies have ardently wooed leading utilities executives and Government officials, have been obliging in helping to arrange US Export-Import Bank credits, and have unstintingly provided technical and material assistance. It still remains to be seen whether the US reactors in Japan will perform according to promise. But the fact remains that the performance of JAPCO's Calder Hall-type reactor has made Japanese utilities extremely reluctant to purchase any more British-made reactors.

When Japan undertook to instal its first commercial atomic power plant in early 1960, the British Atomic Energy Authority had quoted an initial capital cost of around 90 m dollars (£40.5 m) (at current rates). Delays and repairs because of design and mechanical faults ballooned the original cost to 29 m dollars (£53.8 m). At the outset it was estimated that JAPCO 1 would be able to generate power at a cost of around 6.96 dollars (£2.9) per 1,000 kWh. Now it appears the unit would be performing remarkably if the costs could be kept under £5.8 on the average over a five-year period.

By comparison, JAPCO figures its new GE BSR will deliver power at an average of 8.16 dollars (£3.4) per 1,000 kWh over a twenty-year period. And Tokyo Electric with its first BWR and Kansai Electric with its Westinghouse PWR are confident of achieving operating costs in the range originally promised by Japan's one-and-only British-made nuclear reactor. Besides its major emphasis on commercial electric power generation and the new programmes to develop both thermal and fast-breeder reactor prototypes, Japan is proceeding on a broad front to develop atomic energy for peaceful purposes.

In June 1969 Japan launched the hull of its first atomic-powered ship, the 8,350-ton Mutsu, a crew-training and cargo vessel that will be operating in 1972.

The Government is allocating funds for research in the radiological sciences. Japan's iron and steel industry is seeking Government support for development of a dual-purpose reactor that would produce helium at 1,200 degrees Centigrade, the heat being used first in the steelmaking process and then in the production of electric power.

17

Petrochemicals

After World War II Japanese authorities and industrialists realised the importance of building up a strong
petrochemical industry, and in July 1955 the Ministry
of International Trade and Industry announced special
'measures promoting the petrochemical industry'. Japan
has since made spectacular achievements in this field,
and in many petrochemical products Japan's output is
now surpassed only by that of the United States. The
industry's growth continues at a high rate and, in
addition to purely quantitative successes, can be said
to have attained qualitative maturity as well.

Anyone who has visited Japan recently in connection
with the industry will have noticed changes in the
attitudes of leading manufacturers. Whereas until a few
years ago their main preoccupation was with increased
production capacity and markets, they have lately become more cost- and profit-conscious. They are interested in tonnage, but also in the profitability of plants
and of individual products manufactured in those
plants. More importance than in the past is attached to
specialised petrochemicals which offer higher profit
rates, whatever the size of the potential market.

MITI has been playing an important role in this
development. During the period of build-up it granted
tax concessions, special facilities for importing plant

and equipment, and other benefits. The Ministry is supervising the on-stream timing of identical products in different plants in order to avoid market gluts. This has become particularly important with the modern trend towards larger-capacity plants. In the case of ethylene the average plant size under construction is 300,000 tons per annum, compared with 100,000 tons capacity a few years ago, and it is reported that one plant is to have an annual capacity of 500,000 tons. It is estimated that Japan's annual ethylene production (about 1·8 million tons at the beginning of 1968) will reach 3·5 million tons within the next few years. Ethylene output was less than 20,000 tons in 1958.

The production of plastics materials surpassed 3·4 million tons in 1968, an increase of more than 27 per cent over 1967. Output is estimated to be at least 4 million tons in 1969.

Production of synthetic rubber in Japan begun in 1959, reached the level of 100,000 tons in 1963, 200,000 tons in 1966, and over 300,000 tons in 1968. At that time total consumption of new rubber in the country amounted to 602,000 tons, including 257,000 tons natural rubber and 345,000 tons synthetic. The share of synthetic rubbers in this total is increasing steadily despite the geographical proximity of natural rubber sources, and the synthetic rubber industry is at present engaged in further large-scale expansion programmes (including four plants of EPDM rubbers with a total capacity of about 60,000 tons.) The expansion of the motor-car industry (in 1968 4 million units were produced) has resulted in a growing market for tyres and inner tubes, which accounted for nearly 50 per cent of total rubber consumption.

Japan Synthetic Rubber Company, the biggest producer in the industry, was established with a financial participation by the State, but in July 1968 this Government share of about 40 per cent was taken over by the company, so that now it is a fully-owned private company.

Japan is the world's second largest manufacturer of synthetic fibres (being surpassed only by the US), the production of which has steadily increased and diversified. The 1968 output of nylon (over 220,000 tons) will, it is estimated, reach 275,000 tons by 1970; acrylics will increase from 161,000 tons to 216,000 tons; and polyester from 188,000 tons to over 250,000 tons during the same period. The output of polyvinyl alcohol fibres amounted to nearly 70,000 tons in 1968 (a 10 per cent increase over 1967) and is expected to reach 82,000 tons by 1970. These growth rates, moreover, are likely to continue at a higher rate than the overall industrial growth rate.

There are further examples to be quoted in related fields: Japanese authorities have been fostering the research and development of synthetic paper production to curb steadily increasing pulp imports for the rapidly expanding consumption of paper; several factories are under construction to produce synthetic protein from oil for cattle feedstock. This is an important development as Japan imports annually about 9 million tons of animal feedstock; and it must be added that Japan is also a leading manufacturer of ammonia, although very often this industry is dealt with separately in Japanese official statistics and surveys.

The rapid growth of the petrochemical industry has resulted in growing demand for naphtha, which at present accounts for about 10 per cent of the country's total petroleum consumption. In addition, naphtha represents an important feed-stock for town gas and ammonia production (which is not included in the statistics of petrochemicals in Japan), and since 1965 Japan has been importing naphtha from the Middle East.

Japan faces the problem of a steadily increasing shortage of naphtha, while at the same time of not having a sufficiently big market for heavy oils and gasoline. Government-sponsored research is in progress to produce olefins by cracking crude oil (and by using heavy oils for producing petrochemicals). Kureha Chemicals are building an ethylene and acetylene plant by direct cracking of crude oil (Chiyoda Chemical Engineering have been cooperating in this project and also supplying the plant). The question of building up 'chemical refineries' is under consideration, but the utilisation of all by-products would be a serious problem. Investigations are also in progress for establishing ethylene and propylene plants in the oil areas of the [Persian] Gulf, but the difficult shipping problems of these materials would have to be solved. The country's total naphtha consumption will depend on the successful introduction and supply of LNG and LPG to the main gas and electro-power companies, as well as on whether the crude oil hydrogenation process will become a success. This process is in the experimental stages at Osaka Gas and—if successful—could lead to a higher consumption of crude oil at the expense of naphtha.

18

Electronics

More originality in manufacturing techniques is the major aim of Japanese electronics enterprises, encouraged by the Ministry of International Trade and Industry and other relevant authoritative bodies. Japan's rapid surge forward in home and world electronics markets can on the whole be identified with products manufactured using techniques originating elsewhere, generally the United States. Indeed, most Japanese claims to originality have centred around the 'world's first smallest,' or the 'world's first largest' of a proven product. Some developments in 1969 indicated the trend towards new thinking, although the Japanese research involved was not a new idea. One of these was a colour facsimile and telephoto system, developed by Toho Denki Company of Tokyo, which can reproduce original colour from a master photograph for use by newspapers and periodicals.

Toho Denki claims it a world's first with respect to reproducing a colour photograph using a facsimile system. The development is based on what they call a unique scanning, phase synchronisation, and colour compensation system. The company are offering it on world markets now.

Single-gun colour television tube development is another line of research Japanese interests consider possible as a means of obtaining a technological lead, although efforts in this direction by US and European enterprises yielded poor response. Research and development in this direction, headed by Sony TV Picture Tube Development Group, resulted in the introduction in 1969 of the Trinitron colour tube to the UK and US at prices up to 30 per cent cheaper than comparable three-gun domestic tubes. Sony's original development in this product was the Aperture Grille which Sony claims produces a brighter and higher contrast picture. Future research into the construction of the aperture grille is expected to lead to a reduction in circuitry and component complexity of colour television sets.

However, the new thinking now encouraged will be ploughed almost entirely into semiconductor and integrated circuit technology, where Japanese companies pay large sums in royalties and manufacturing licences. Some results of this research are expected as exhibits at EXPO '70.

Latest advances in colour television set technology are being brought about more by necessity than aspirations towards higher scientific endeavour. Production targets for 1969, set at 4 million sets, began floundering because of a rundown of vacuum tube production resulting from wide scale applications of semiconductors. Crash developments into production of all-semiconductor sets were ordered. The Japanese market for colour television was still buoyant in 1969, although somewhat inflated by a new demand for video tape recorders. Nevertheless, it was expected to fall short of the 1968 peak. In 1968 colour television production accounted for one-third of total consumer electronics. MITI figures indicate that 2,740,000 sets were produced worth 79 m dollars (£33 m)—a 114 per cent increase over 1967. Of these 70 per cent were 19-inch sets, but in 1969 the sale of 17- and 13-inch sets was expected to increase appreciably.

To cope with the 1969 demand makers in 1968

expanded plant and facilities, but by May of 1969 it was estimated that sales targets would not be attained on the home market and efforts were made to increase the export percentage. These export drives are being hampered by pending anti-dumping measures in the US—60 per cent of Japanese colour television exports —and a cutback in US spending in Vietnam, reducing consumer spending in South-east Asia and Korea, Japan's other major export outlet. A new spearhead is scheduled for Australia, where the PAL system will be broadcast about the end of 1971. Matsushita Electrical Industries have already established a plant in Australia with this aim and two other manufacturers are expected to follow suit in 1970.

The most significant development in the computer industry, already in the proposal stage by the Ministry of International Trade and Industry, is a plan to establish a government-subsidised software development group, labelled the 'System Technology Development Centre'. When in operation in 1970 it will form the basis for building sophisticated applications packages —products virtually non-existent in Japanese computer manufacturing industry.

The concept of the plan suggests that the key objective is to create packages independently of foreign enterprises and to enable Japanese experts to participate directly in large-scale nationally orientated projects. Basic funding for the centre will be 6 m dollars (£2.5 m) of which 3.6 m dollars (£1.5 m) will be subsidised by the Government. Initially 200 researchers will be engaged in projects, and eventually 1,000 researchers will be recruited. Annual costs to run the centre will be 24 m dollars (£10 m).

Overall production of electronic products in Japan in 1968 amounted to 5,352 m dollars (£2,230 m), compared with 3,888 m dollars (£1,620 m) in 1967, and is estimated to reach 6,888 m dollars (£2,870 m) in 1969. Exports in 1968 amounted to 1,392 m dollars (£580 m), compared with 1,008 m dollars (£420 m) in 1967, and are estimated to reach 1,536 m dollars (£640 m) in 1969.

Production of integrated circuits reached 20 million pieces in 1968. Output of thick and thin films reached 25 million. Total integrated circuit production was estimated at 24 m dollars (£10 m). Of the total, digital circuits amounted to 10·6 million units, linear circuits amounted to 1·4 million units, and MOS circuits amounted to 7·8 million. Production of MOS circuits, used mainly in desk top calculators, accounted for 39·5 per cent of the total semiconductor output.

19

Consumer goods

The Japanese worker would, if politeness permitted, raise an incredulous eyebrow if one suggested to him that he was an affluent member of an affluent society. But even he would find it difficult to explain away the very visible evidence that this is fast becoming the case. Business in the department stores in Tokyo, Osaka and other major cities, and also in all the smaller towns, is booming; supermarkets are proliferating and the leisure industry, catering for the feverish zeal with which the Japanese engage in everything from golf to ski-ing, from motoring to mountaineering, is growing at a pace that exhausts all the superlatives. The thriftiness of the Japanese remains unimpaired: family savings averaged some 3,360 dollars (£1,400) at the end of 1968, a 22 per cent increase on the previous year. Yet over the same period department stores sales increased by 20 per cent.

The phenomenon is a reflection of various factors. Salaries and wages have risen substantially; the majority of employees receive a twice-yearly bonus equivalent to three or four months' earnings: increasing numbers of women, both single and married, are working and contributing to the family income. This has not passed unremarked upon by Japanese manufacturers who are more than prepared not only to cater for existing demand for consumer goods, but to add continuously to their range.

Exporters of consumer goods to Japan have an advantage over their domestic competitors—foreignness. The peculiar attraction that foreignness exerts manifests itself in a thousand and one ways. Many of them are apparent to the most superficial observer since they are expressed in the English language. 'Peace', 'Hope' and 'Fuji' are popular brands of cigarettes, so called and so labelled. The great majority of Japan's nightclubs and bars have English (or French) names— and not because they are catering for the tourists, who form a very small proportion of their clientele. Japanese advertisers who wish to strike a prestige or 'snob appeal' note will often use as a copy headline an 'English' phrase such as 'Good Show' or 'Jolly Fine' and pose their models against a backcloth reminiscent more of gracious living in Britain or America than of their own country.

The appeal of foreign goods and the prestige that attaches to them has its roots in the Meiji era when, little more than a hundred years ago, Japan broke out of the cocoon of centuries to discover and desire the bewildering variety of Western products revealed to them—and to accord them a reputation that has persisted through succeeding generations. Persisted and, in the years that have followed World War II, been augmented by the ever-increasing adoption in material terms and at all levels of society of Western modes and manners.

It can be seen in the accelerating trend among the younger executives to Western style furniture and furnishings for their homes and in their acquisition of sophisticated gadgetry for their leisure pursuits. It can be seen in the increasing amount of display space being accorded to foreign consumer goods in the windows and on the counters of stores and shops. It can be seen most strikingly in the attention such displays receive on the two annual gift-giving seasons that mark the Japanese year. Then indeed, within the upper levels of the carefully graduated scales of value and importance the Japanese apply on these occasions, foreign goods are in high demand.

20

Cameras

Few people would dispute that cameras have become one of the most typical prestige symbols of industrial Japan. A large proportion of the satin chrome, leatherette and glass in any Western photographic dealer's window comes from Japan, and even the photographically uninformed know that the era of the cheap Japanese copy is long since dead. Today's models are original in design, equipped with sophisticated mechanisms and outstanding optics, and in many cases embody a sizeable electronics content for such purposes as precise exposure determination. Moreover, a significant percentage represent the top end of the camera price bracket. Quality, not price, has become the new selling point, backed by an independently administered random testing programme instituted by the Government to maintain export standards.

Japanese cameras come in a wide range of shapes and sizes, but the scene-stealer, the camera type which epitomises Japanese design and which has become the photographic hall-mark of the 1960s, is unquestionably the 35 mm single-lens reflex, better known simply as the SLR. SLR cameras embody a distinctive and accurate viewing and focusing system, in which the taking lens is at the same time the viewing lens, via a mirror, screen, and pentaprism combination. This means that the image in the viewfinder is a perfect preview in framing and focus of the final picture.

The advantages that this type confers are numerous, and with very few exceptions it has superseded all other in the higher price bracket. Since it is at the same time the most logical camera type to employ in conjunction with interchangeable lenses, it has also greatly benefited the Japanese optical industry, and the concept of the SLR as the basis of a complete photographic system has largely taken over from the old idea of the camera as a self-sufficient unit. Interchangeable lenses, close-up attachments, bellows units and other ancillary apparatus extend the already impressive versatility of the SLR still further, and have opened up an additional and very healthy sphere of export business.

In 1968 Japanese still camera production figures totalled 4,139,177 pieces, valued at 161.7 m dollars (£67 m) of which 2,316,694 pieces were for export, valued at 94.2 m dollars (£39 m). Comparable figures for SLR (focal plane shutter) cameras were (production) 1,109,730 pieces, value 81.9 m dollars and (export) 715,202 pieces, value 53.3 m dollars (£22 m). Thus it will be seen that although the SLR exports in terms of units came to roughly one-third of the total still camera export figure, in terms of value they account for over half. Compared with 1967 the growth rate for SLR exports was 131·8 per cent, a very marked advance. Grand total figures, including cine products and interchangeable lenses were (production) 5,970,895, value 236.7 m dollars (£99 m), and (export) 3,523,871, value 143 m dollars (£60 m).

Much of the rise to fame of Japanese cameras is due to the outstanding reputation of their lenses, which exhibit the requisite characteristics of high contrast, razor-sharp delineation, and freedom from light scatter even at wide apertures. The problems of optical design have been increasingly taken over by computers, speeding up the output rate (work previously involving weeks of calculation now takes a matter of hours) and

116

ensuring consistent quality. As a result recent introductions include the quantity production of very wide
aperture lenses incorporating aspherical elements
which are beneficial to definition and eliminate flare
and similar aberrations, but which have hitherto been
extremely costly and time-consuming to manufacture
even in small numbers. Another innovation has been a
lens utilising elements made of fluorite. Such lenses can
be of simpler construction, afford improved correc-
tions, are smaller and lighter (a valuable attribute in
the case of telephoto designs of 300 mm focal length and
above), and have much greater light transmission
properties. In more conventional optics there is a great
variety from which to choose for each SLR—one company offers no less than thirty—from ultra-wide angle
and fisheye lenses of 180 degrees to super telephoto
mirror designs of 1,000 mm and more, adaptable to
virtually every photographic task. In addition, some
companies are specialist lens manufacturers, making no
camera themselves but lenses with adapters to suit
most available camera bodies.

Although the 35 mm SLR is the predominant type,
the industry caters for every taste and requirement,
with models from 16 mm subminiatures to press and
technical cameras. One make is unique, a twin-lens
reflex with interchangeable optics, and new 'compact'
cameras are now appearing to meet the fashion for full-
frame 35 mm models which will slip easily into a pocket
or handbag. Japanese cameras have been into space
with the American astronauts, and one piece of apparatus, the Minolta Space Meter exposure meter, is
standard equipment on the Apollo missions.

Inevitably, with the Japanese opting out of the cheap
end of the market, other countries have not been slow
to move in, and Hong Kong has become a large-scale
supplier of the simple fixed-focus type of camera. As
well as the established West German competition,
Japan has to face the challenge of well-built, medium-
to low-priced cameras from Eastern Europe, notably

East Germany and the Soviet Union, which have entered the market in increasing numbers as Japanese products have become more sophisticated.

While the industry is now fairly well entrenched in its leading position, the Japanese have always taken a long-term view of their markets (their policy of ensuring that there are adequate provisions for after-sales service of their products is one instance), and many camera companies are now extending their manufactured range by diversifying into related fields such as microfilm equipment, office machinery, such as copiers and calculators, and medical-optical apparatus. With the photographic industry coming to depend more and more on electronics, and in consequence moving out of its hitherto closely defined limits, it will indeed be interesting to watch its progress over the next few years.

21

Textiles

Since 1952 the Japanese textile industry, taken as a whole, has exhibited the kind of progress that the West has come to associate with the Japanese economy generally. However, the overall upward trend in output conceals some marked changes in its composition, and some quite painful structural reorganisation.

The figures for production and exports themselves go a long way towards revealing the progress and prospects of the industry. After almost a decade of steady growth the output of cotton yarn reached a peak of just over 550,000 metric tons in 1960, and after a considerable falling off in the early 1960s this figure was not again attained until 1968. Production of cotton fabrics has not regained the peak of 3,221 million square metres produced in 1960, and the trend continues downwards, albeit slowly. Again, the trend in exports of cotton yarn and fabric has been downward throughout the 1960s, both in value and quantity. Cotton yarn exports in 1968 (7,006 metric tons) were 13·7 per cent greater than the bad year of 1967, but more than 50 per cent down on the figures for 1966 (15,822 metric tons). Export of cotton fabrics was down by 17 per cent in 1968 compared with 1967.

In the even older silk industry rising domestic demand has pressed against a production level which has been fairly constant for about ten years. As a result exports have been falling constantly in volume and value, with declines particularly marked in the important North American market.

The picture is very similar in the case of rayon, with output of spun rayon yarn barely establishing a fresh peak in the late 1960s after falling off in the early 1960s and spun viscose rayon cloth production, for example, holding fairly constant around 900 million square metres, but well below its peak of 1,057 million square metres in 1960. In the export field, spun rayon yarn fell by 9·3 per cent in 1968, while spun rayon fabric exports were down 15·7 per cent in quantity compared with 1967.

In addition, Japan became a net importer of cotton yarn for the first time in 1967, mainly due to a sharp rise in imports from Pakistan, while the import quantity in 1968 (14,771 metric tons) was 41·5 per cent up on 1967. Imports of cotton fabrics were 159·3 per cent greater in 1968 than in the previous year and the likely trend is upward, although the figure is, as yet, well below that for exports.

The successes scored by the industry in recent years have come on two main overlapping fronts; first, in the rapid increase in the production and export of synthetic fibres and fabrics, and secondly in the production and export of made-up goods of all kinds. For example, spun synthetic yarn production stood at 368,412 metric tons in 1968 representing a 20·3 per cent increase over the previous year. Its output has overtaken that of spun rayon yarn and its growth indicates that it may soon overtake cotton yarn in the place of primacy. Of the total synthetic yarn produced nearly three-quarters was of the polyester and acrylic type, with polyester the largest individual category. Spun synthetic fabric production stood at 1,049 million square metres in 1968, an increase of 8·5 per cent over the 1967 figure, while production of cotton and spun viscose rayon fabrics had fallen. Exports of spun synthetic yarn, notably of the acrylic type, rose by 68·7 per cent to 34,757 metric tons in 1968, while spun synthetic fabrics, mostly of the polyester blended with cotton or rayon staple type, increased by 30·5 per cent over the 1967 figure of 524 million square metres. Exports of all kinds of made-up goods showed improvement in 1968 and continue to do so this year, but here again the most marked improvements have come in the man-made fibre sector.

The trends towards the production and export of more capital-intensive, technically sophisticated kinds of textile goods are well understood by Japanese manufacturers. While complaining, as the chairman of the Japan Spinner's Association did in 1969, of the use of export incentives by developing countries' textile industries in contravention of the spirit of GATT arrangements, concrete adjustment measures are being taken.

A law was passed in 1967 to encourage the disposal of redundant machinery, the modernisation of equipment, and the attainment of a more optimum size of enterprise. The results so far have been the scrapping of about 800,000 spindles, 671,000 compulsorily. This represents about 7 per cent of current spinning capacity, while at the same time loom capacity was reduced by 3 per cent in 1968 over the 1967 figure.

Enough rationalisation of this harsh but realistic kind has taken place to allow the legal ban on the installation of new spinning machines to be lifted from July 1970, and in the face of an ever-growing concern with the acute labour shortage and consequent rapid increases in wages, the emphasis from now on will be firmly on the modernisation of existing equipment, progress towards a more complete adoption of the three shift system with the continuous automated spinning system, and such innovational technology as the open-end spinning machine.

While having to face the cold wind of competition from the industries of the emergent Asian nations in the more traditional branches of textile production, and having to adjust painfully to it, and having moved towards a position of dominance in the Asian markets as far as synthetic fibres and made-up goods are concerned, the Japanese industry views with some concern what it regards as the restrictive measures imposed against it by the EEC countries in particular, and with some annoyance the recently declared desire of the American industry to conclude voluntary export restraint agreements in man-made fibres and wool products, particularly as the US industry has of recent years experienced comparative prosperity.

22

Housing

One of the most notable exceptions to tremendous improvements in the general Japanese standard of living is housing. Many Japanese are still badly under-housed. One-room families, which symbolise the present housing problem in Japan, total in numbers between 250,000 and 500,000 in each major metropolitan area. Poor housing conditions seem endemic to modern Japan, despite an average annual economic growth rate of over 9 per cent.

One out of every six Japanese families is inadequately housed. Millions of families live in 'non-residence' type company dormitories and additional millions share small homes with other families (usually close relatives). Most Japanese houses require immediate and costly repairs. Few are anything but exceptionally small by Western housing criteria. The problem has reached semi-crisis proportions, with an estimated 48 per cent of Japanese families intensely dissatisfied with housing conditions. Yet the majority of Japanese families are resigned to the necessity for patience until the Government can develop an adequate programme to relieve the situation.

Acute housing difficulties have been largely ignored by the Government in recent years. What little has been done has been unimaginative. However, on 8 September,

1969, the Japanese Construction Ministry created a research committee to study possibilities of encouraging private housing construction. The committee will concern itself with home building land tract development, the creation of a 'real estate trust system', under which farmland owners in the suburbs of Japan's largest cities will cooperate with trust banks and building contractors in the building of residential houses. Measures will also be taken to improve the present Governmental credit supplementing system for private housing construction financing through the nation's Housing Finance Corporation. It is considered likely that a new private insurance system will be introduced for assisting the wealthy property insurance companies to provide a large share of such financing. Finally, the committee will study plans for a governmental interest-paying subsidy system for bank loans for private homes and small-scale housing developments of approximately fifty family apartments.

Apartment block designed by Kunio Maekawa; traditional housing in a village near Hiroshima.

In 1969, the Industrial Structure Council urged the Ministry of International Trade and Industry to develop a programme under which the Government could assist in the consolidation of Japan's fledgling prefabricated housing industry. Government encouragement could improve financial, technological and sales conditions which would make available to Japanese families much less expensive but high quality prefabricated homes on a large-scale basis. With such Government aid, the council noted, the small-capacity prefabricated housing industry could play a more extensive role in providing hundreds of thousands of new homes.

These two latest moves towards possible relief for cramped Japanese families depend to a considerable extent for eventual success on the Government's national budget for fiscal 1970, a document expected to place new emphasis on housing problems. Still it is very unlikely that more than 1·7 million new homes and apartments will be constructed in 1970. These would include both national and local government and private housing projects. Programmes for 1969 probably did not result in construction of more than 1,550,000 dwellings (counting individual apartments as a single home). Annual demand in Japan is considered much higher than these figures indicate.

One important category of new housing is largely omitted from the official figures. This consists of houses built by families which have become exasperated with the Government's failure to launch a meaningful building programme and constructed homes in suburbs as much as one-and-a-half to two hours or more travel time from city centres. What these families were looking for was land cheap enough to match their savings. Scarcity of in-city land has sent real estate values skyrocketing over the last decade. The average land price index number as at March reached 1,165, according to the Japan Real Estate Research Institute, which uses a base index figure of 100 set in March 1955.

The average price of one independent housing unit on a building site of 110 square metres and with a floor space of about 65 square metres is somewhere between 13,500 dollars (£5,625) and 16,000 dollars (£6,670), provided it is not located in choice metropolitan areas. In fifteen years the cost is expected to rise beyond 102,000 dollars (£42,500). Land prices and scarcity of available sites in urban areas and the resulting soaring costs of single homes is causing the Japanese to concentrate on high-rise apartment construction.

Housing experts of the Sanwa Bank of Osaka believe that the nation cannot limit apartment structures to those below ten storeys if rentals and outright purchase of individual units is to be kept within reach of working-class incomes. But the problem, according to real estate firms, is that if prefabrication is to be considered it may be technically impossible to build such structures higher than ten or twelve storeys. In recent years precast concrete sections have been used in Japan for construction of three- to five-storey apartment buildings—and hundreds of de luxe apartment structures have been erected in the same manner up to eight and ten storeys high. The answer would seem to lie in the plans of some of the more than 120 Japanese companies in the building prefabrication field that are experimenting with steel and plastic frames and walls. Success in this area could greatly reduce construction costs, which have been rising by about 10 to 15 per cent yearly. Prefabrication tends to slash labour requirements, now running at approximately 30 per cent of housing construction costs. All these considerable problems will have to be solved if Japan is to avoid becoming a nation of one-room families.

JAPAN
politics
and history

Students of engineering in India with their instructor from Japan.

23

Outline history

Tradition relates that in 660 BC Jimmu Tenno, descendant of the Sun Goddess, founded the Japanese Empire and the Imperial line which descends to the Emperor Hirohito today.

There has always been an Emperor in Japan, though few have ruled. The Emperor was sacrosanct, primarily because of his divinity in Shinto ('The Way of the Gods'). The original ritualistic religion of Japan, Shinto survived through many permutations to be re-established as a national cult in the 1870s. Buddhism came from Korea with Chinese writing, silk manufacture and other inestimable influences in the fifth to sixth centuries AD, and has coexisted with Shinto ever since.

Prince Shotoku Taishi (d. AD 621)—a major force behind Buddhism and Chinese influence in general—and Fujiwara Kamatari (in Japan family names are placed before personal names) whose clan governed for over three centuries after his death, remodelled Japanese clan-organised society on the Chinese T'ang Empire: they established a complex centralised administration—a formula which foundered on the power individual clans derived from their provincial isolation in a mountainous country. The most lasting achievement of the Fujiwara period was perhaps the Heian culture, and the tradition of artistic leadership at the political centre which continued throughout the subsequent centuries of military rule and even through the anarchy

Buddha: the thirteenth-century statue at Kamakura.

of the fourteenth-sixteenth centuries.

In the twelfth century the Fujiwara clan split, and the subsequent struggle for power threw up the shogunate: military dictatorship in the name of the Emperor by successive members of the same clan. This form of government lasted until the Meiji Restoration (1868). It was reasonably effective in 1185–1339, but 1339–1573 was a period of continual violence, though also of commercial progress; the shogun alone lived in calm and aesthetic splendour at his court in Heiankyo (Kyoto).

In 1549 St Francis Xavier landed in Japan. First contacts with the West involved trade, guns, and Christianity—which, with government support, spread rapidly.

Between 1568 and 1616 Japan was reunited and order restored. The last of the triumvirate who achieved this founded the Tokugawa Shogunate (1615–1868) and established a feudal form of government whose aim was to maintain the *status quo* and the dominant position of the Tokugawa family. All military lords (*daimyo*) were required to participate in expensive ceremonies and to attend the shogunal court regularly, leaving their families as hostages when they returned to their provincial estates. In order to prevent an alliance between dissident *daimyo* and foreigners, the frontiers were closed, Europeans driven from the country (except for Deshima, the Dutch trading post in Nagasaki) and Christianity was made illegal. The result was peace for 250 years.

Paradoxically the military ethic was supreme, though its practice was confined to the samurai class. But peace, the economic burdens of the *daimyo* and the social taboo on commercialism fostered the position of the merchants—socially and politically the dregs of the rigid class system. Money finally replaced rice as the tool of exchange, and the tensions arising from a money economy in a society where gain was a contemptible aspiration proved incapable of governmental cure. By the mid-nineteenth century Tokugawa power was weakening. The American Commodore Perry (1853–54) and Western intrusion applied the *coup de grace*, and the shogunate was abolished in favour of Imperial government.

The Meiji Restoration (1868) was symbolised by the nobility's voluntary surrender of their territories to the Emperor. The country was divided into administrative units—prefectures—and the class hierarchy abolished. The samurai lost their monopoly of military service. The primary aim of the outstanding young statesmen of this period was to overthrow the humiliating Western trade treaties of the 1850s. Influenced by China's failure, they adopted the barbarians' own weapons: industrialisation, financed from rural taxes; a modern nationwide army; and constitutional government. The 1889 constitution established a Diet but left real responsibility in the hands of the Emperor and the cabinet he appointed. Universal male suffrage came only in 1925.

Japan's military successes against China (1894–95) and Russia (1904–5) registered the success of westernisation. Japan joined the Allies in 1914 and ended the war with new territory, in China and the Pacific islands.

In the 1920s apparent progress towards liberal democracy disguised fundamental problems: in particular the power of the army in politics and the association of politicians and parties with big business. Political corruption, the Depression (especially through the slump in American demand for silk) and tension between the advancing Kuo-Mintang and the Japanese forces in Manchuria combined to throw Japan into the hands of the military who were increasingly controlled by an extremist wing. In 1931 the Manchurian Incident launched a policy of military expansion in Asia which escalated into the Pacific War against the United States.

After her defeat Japan was occupied from 1945 to 1952, when the treaty of San Francisco re-established her sovereignty.

In modern Japan, the Emperor has no legislative power. This resides in the Diet, made up of an Upper

Traditional samurai costume is worn at the annual festival of archery and horsemanship held at Kamakura since 1172.

and a Lower House. Half of the 250 members of the House of Councillors (Upper House) are elected every three years. The forty-six Prefectural Districts elect 150 members and 100 members are elected at large. There

Prime Minister Sato addresses a meeting of the Liberal Democratic Party.

are 486 seats in the House of Representatives (Lower House), whose members are elected for not more than four years. The House of Representatives is the more powerful body; it controls the Budget and approves treaties with foreign powers.

Executive power is vested in the Cabinet, which is collectively responsible to the Diet. Prime Ministers must be civilians. Japan's main political parties are the Liberal Democrat Party the Komeito, the Japan Socialist Party, the Democratic Socialist Party, and the Communist Party. The ruling Liberal Democratic Party is business-oriented, influenced at the national level by big business, at the local level by small and medium-size business and farm groups. On domestic policy, the LDP is moderately conservative. In foreign policy, the majority of the LDP is pro-Western but a growing minority within the party favours a slightly more neutralist stance with less dependence upon the United States, and eventual recognition of Peking. The LDP has stayed in power since the opposition parties offer no responsible alternatives.

The Japan Socialist Party is still wedded to a doctrinaire Marxism, and efforts by its leaders to move towards a more pragmatic programme are not making much headway. The party appears to be on the decline. The Democratic Socialist Party, Japan's third most important political organisation, follows a non-Marxist socialist line but lacks attractive leadership and programmes that can make an impact on the public.

The Komeito (Clean Government) Party, the political arm of the Buddhist Soka Gakkai Sect, is a political organ looking for a programme. The policy measures it has adopted are oriented to the lower middle class and workers in small business and to a neutralist foreign policy.

The LDP, barring serious blunders or economic difficulties of a serious nature, can expect to hold power for some time to come. The JSP is in a state of decline. Komeito and the DSP may make modest gains in future elections. The JCP is well organised, still growing slowly, but unlikely to achieve anything politically unless a general breakdown occurs.

24

Student unrest

During the past four years well over a hundred of the 845 universities and colleges in Japan, among them many of the largest and most influential in the country, have been disrupted by strikes and violence. The immediate causes of the disputes have varied: at Waseda, an increase in fees and disagreement over the management of a new student hostel; at Keio, the university's acceptance of contract-work for the United States armed forces; at Tokyo University, the internship system for medical students. But these are merely the sparks that have set off the explosions. The underlying cause of the unrest is the extreme overcrowding that has prevented many universities from fulfilling their functions.

For the academic year 1968–69, 1·27 million students were enrolled at universities offering four-year courses and 255,000 at junior colleges offering two- or three-year courses, a total of over 1·5 million. This represents an increase of nearly 10 per cent over the previous year, and of 130 per cent over 1958.

Most Japanese universities are private institutions which, since government support is negligible, must rely on bank loans, donations, contract-work and tuition fees for their income. There is thus a great deal of pressure on them to take more and more students without a proportionate increase in their expenditure on facilities such as libraries, which in many universities are totally inadequate.

A university degree is vitally important to the young Japanese who wishes to make a career in the bureaucracy or in one of the large companies that offer lifetime security to their employees. Since both the ministries and the largest companies normally recruit almost exclusively from one or two universities with which they have particularly close connections, there is intense competition for places in the dozen or so most prestigious universities. High schools are judged by the number of students they send to the top universities, middle schools by the number of pupils they send to the best high schools. Many children spend all their evenings from the age of seven or eight doing home-work or taking extra tuition (often, ironically, from university students) in order to improve their chances of getting into the right schools.

When they finally arrive at university they find that it is often impossible to find a seat for lectures they are required to attend, that they have no personal contact with their teachers (who usually have part-time jobs at three or four other universities, and who may simply fail to turn up for one class out of four), and that they have to work in their own (frequently shared) rooms or queue for seats in the public libraries. The resulting frustration and resentment mean that politically active students are able to gain considerable support for campaigns for 'democratisation of the campus' and redress of grievances. However, the activists have gone much further in both their aims and their methods than the vast majority of students are willing to follow.

The organised student movement in Japan is based on the *jichikai*, or self-government association. The student is usually enrolled automatically in the *jichikai* of his faculty. The university often collects his sub-scription together with his tuition fees and hands it over to the officers of the association. The *jichikai* are affiliated to the Zengakuren (All Japan Federation of Student Self-Government Associations). The Zengakuren was founded in 1948, and from then until the end of the 1950s virtually all its officers, at national and at university level, were members of the Communist Party, but the dissatisfaction of the more radical elements with the Central Committee's 'Right-wing opportunism' and lack of revolutionary zeal led to a split in the years 1958–60.

The movement is now broadly divided into a 'pro-

Students celebrate their coming of age on Adults' Day, 15 January.

Yoyogi' faction (the headquarters of the Japan Communist Party are at Yoyogi in Tokyo), which still controls about 65 per cent of the *jichikai*, and an 'anti-Yoyogi' faction, which is further subdivided into a huge number of sects roughly classifiable as Maoist, Trotskyite and Structural Reformist. Most of the violence that has occurred on university campuses has arisen from the rivalry between the pro- and anti-Yoyogi factions and among the various anti-Yoyogi sects. At Tokyo University, for example, anti-Yoyogi groups occupied part of the campus, whereupon the pro-Yoyogi faction occupied the rest. This situation persisted for half a year, during which time 'confrontations' took place on several occasions between armies several thousand strong of armed and helmeted students. Eventually, the university authorities called in the riot-police, who were only able to evict the diehards after a two-day siege of their last strong-hold, the university auditorium, in the course of which hundreds of Molotov cocktails were thrown by the students and hundreds of tear-gas grenades fired by the police.

The most appalling aspect of this war among the students is the brutal treatment of prisoners. Members of rival factions have frequently been seized and subjected to severe beatings, and many have been very seriously injured.

The radical students use the university campuses as fortresses from which they make forays into the streets to demonstrate violently against the American presence in Okinawa or the Security Treaty between Japan and the United States. They have attempted on several occasions to turn the whole of the *'karuchie ratan'* (Quartier Latin—the Kanda district in Tokyo, where there are several universities) into a 'liberated area', throwing up barricades across the streets. The government has since taken powers which will enable it to impose sanctions on teachers who do not cooperate with university authorities in settling disputes. Universities disrupted by disputes for more than nine months can be closed. All students and university teachers are united in regarding this as a threat to academic freedom. Not only the content of the Act giving the Government the necessary powers, but also the manner in which it was passed has aroused indignation. The Act has exacerbated rather than relieved the situation.

The real losers in all this, of course, are the students and teachers who want to see reform in the universities, but have instead seen them virtually destroyed by radical students, and are now faced with what they regard, not without reason, as the threat of dictation to the universities by a Government whose interference in education they regard with apprehension.

25

Foreign relations

In the years since the accession to office of Prime Minister Sato in 1964 the Asian scene and Japan's position have been transformed. This transformation has presented Japan with the need for new diplomatic emphases and adjustments which may be of significance to powers on all sides of the Pacific Ocean.

In the past five years President Sukarno has fallen from power, China has experienced the Cultural Revolution, fighting has occurred between Russia and China, and the British Government has planned its withdrawal from East of Suez. But overshadowing all these significant changes has been the Vietnam War and its impact on President Nixon's Asian diplomacy. In this context of instability, change, and painful rethinking Japan can well be seen as a haven of economic progress, growing strength, and political continuity. Her economy has continued to boom, her exports have reached 13,000 m dollars (£5,416 m), and with the production of Uranium 235 she has the capability, if not the aim, of constructing nuclear weapons.

Besides these physical achievements Japan has also shown increasing signs of diplomatic self-assertion; in response to popular feeling the Liberal Democratic Government regained control of the Bonin Islands, and began pressing the United States to restore Japanese administration to Okinawa and the rest of the Ryukyu group. Many Japanese would prefer the restoration of Okinawa with no strings attached, but a compromise including the continuation of American bases may well be the outcome of projected talks.

Arduous negotiations over Okinawa and American unhappiness at her £416 m (990.5 m dollars) trade deficit with Japan should not be seen as evidence of a fundamental change in relations between Washington and Tokyo. The Japanese Government continues to base its defence upon the Security Treaty with the United States, and with over a quarter of her exports going to the American market Japan is highly dependent on American prosperity and liberal trading policies. Indeed protectionist policies in the United States and other advanced countries could be politically and economically damaging to Japan's development. For if Japan's living standards do not continue to rise the resulting frustration could endanger political stability.

While Japan's increasing strength has produced some friction in the US, other changes, some in American policy, have brought Japan significant advantages. The growing Sino-Soviet rift has strengthened Russia's fear of China and softened Moscow's attitude towards Japan, while America's desire for a *détente* with the Soviet Union has eased the way for Japan to respond to Russia's moves. Besides abating her active hostility Russia now feels that she can gain from cooperating with Japan in the economic development of her exposed Eastern territories; in August 1968 Japan agreed to join in the development of lumbering in West Siberia, the Japan-Soviet Economic Committee is surveying the resources of South Siberia and Sakhalin, and the Moscow–Tokyo air service is to be improved and extended. There is still, however, no peace treaty between Japan and the Soviet Union, and Japan's claims to the islands of Habomai, Shikotan, Etorofu and Kunashiri are still unanswered. But even friction on these rather emotive issues can hardly halt the momentum of trade and economic cooperation.

While Japan's relations with Russia have improved in recent years relations with mainland China have been almost paralysed by the Cultural Revolution. In the early summer of 1966 prominent spokesmen in Japan's ruling party were urging the Cabinet to make new moves towards diplomatic recognition of Peking. And this pressure, combined with the hopes of Japanese business men, seemed to point towards increasing links with the Chinese Government. But the new Chinese militancy which accompanied the Cultural Revolution suddenly froze Sino-Japanese relations in their existing limited form. In 1968 the existing private trade agreement was only extended for one further year and this actually envisaged a contraction of 33 m dollars (£14 m) in this relatively limited trade. As China has returned to less turbulent conditions Japanese statements have acquired a more flexible and positive nature. And despite China's attempt to extract political concessions for the continuation of trade, Japanese speeches have contained an interesting mixture of old and novel elements. The traditional theme of 'the separation of politics from economics' (which permits diplomatic relations with Taiwan and trade with the mainland) has been combined with patient talk of 'restoring China's confidence in Japan step by step' and the Japanese Foreign Minister has mentioned the possibility of a Tokyo–Peking air link. 'The flight of a Chinese ballet company' was the first step suggested in this connection but the broader implication was clear. Japan has also shown growing willingness to ease the financing of trade with the Communist regime.

In 1964 the Yoshida Letter assured the Taiwan Government that Japanese Import–Export Bank credits would not be made available to finance trade with the Peking Government but although this is still the general principle underpinning Japanese policy it is now stated that such credits may be granted on 'a case-by-case basis'. This gesture should not be understood as a serious cooling of attitude towards Taiwan, which Japan sees as a vital area, but nevertheless it marks an attempt to move forward from the sterile rigid pattern of recent years. Though trade with Peking cannot hope to replace that with the advanced and affluent states of the West, improved relations with a nuclear China are desirable for any Japanese Government; and at a time when American attitudes towards Peking are apparently more flexible it seems more likely than ever that there will be some slow improvement in relations across the China Sea.

While turmoil in China has stunted the development of Sino-Japanese relations, the fall of President Sukarno has aided the development of contacts with Indonesia. The decline of Communist influence and the return to financial orthodoxy have both led to stronger diplomatic and economic links between Tokyo and Djakarta. Besides her obvious interest in a stable regime in Indonesia, Japan has much to gain in the future from the exploitation of Indonesia's raw materials. And already these factors have produced increased Japanese investment in Indonesian oil and timber, a 100 m dollar (£42 m) loan to the Suharto Government, and Japanese technical assistance in rice farming and fisheries.

Undoubtedly the most politically taxing problem for Japan in recent years has been the Vietnam war. On the one hand, as a close economic and military partner of the US the Japanese Government has felt compelled to give moral support to the American military effort. On the other, Japanese public opinion, fearing the escalation of the war into a Sino-American nuclear conflict, has been strongly opposed to the whole tenor of American policy. It is true that Japan has made economic gains by supplying material for the American forces, but a series of disturbing incidents, including a local rise in radioactivity after the visit of an American nuclear submarine, further intensified the fears of many Japanese. This widespread popular alarm must have been among the reasons for America's decision to transfer a number of her installations to Japanese control.

Meanwhile the Japanese Government, apprehensive at the apparent instability of South-east Asia, and concerned to support American policy, has played an increasingly active role in the region. Prime Minister Sato has embarked on sweeping tours of South-east Asia and Australasia, the Thai Prime Minister has been welcomed to Japan, and Japan has played an active role in ASPAC and the Asian Development Bank. Japan has had defence talks with Australia, given increased aid and investment to South Korea and played a far more active part in non-military regional organisations than at any other time since 1945.

This increased activity is not surprising, for it is perhaps among the small and under-developed states of South-east Asia that Japan's power has most room for manoeuvre. Certainly the United States would approve of a more active Japanese role in this area, but the problems involved should not be minimised. President Nixon, determined to avoid another Vietnam war and hoping to reduce the American commitment, has spoken of 'peace in Asia coming primarily from the initiative of those who live in Asia', and some observers believe that America would like to see Japan play a more active military role in South-east Asia, but so far Japan has rejected the idea of entering regional alliances. Japan's position is delicate and understandable, for many doubts surround an over-hasty acceptance of the American torch.

Japan is still a relatively poor country when compared to America or the richer European states, and a big diversion of resources to military or overseas spending might well be damaging to the improvement of social services at home. Furthermore, Japan is a country where anti-military feeling and pacifism are a very real element in public opinion, and while many Japanese accept the existence of Japanese armed forces many might be severely shaken by the clear acceptance of military commitments overseas. Such a departure might further deepen the gulf which separates Government and Opposition and this could hardly be beneficial to parliamentary government. Finally, too heavy a foreign presence, whether commercial or military, could in time provoke a nationalistic reaction in South-east Asia, and this could ultimately do great harm to the development of the region.

Japan has valuable know-how and capital which can assist the development of her southern neighbours but it would be wrong to overestimate the resources at her command or to disregard the frictions and domestic repercussions which might stem from too rapid a change of course.

26

Foreign aid

Japan has had the reputation ever since its postwar resurgence of being less generous than most other major industrial nations with its foreign aid, and more inclined than most to harness the aid which it does give to commercial ends. To suggest that this reputation is undeserved would be to fly directly in the face of figures which, for most of the sixties, show Japan as charging high interest rates by the standards of other donor countries, and offering only a small proportion of its total aid in the form of non-repayable grants. But it would be equally unfair to maintain that the officials and politicians concerned with the programme are unaware of or unconcerned by its failings. The truth is that foreign aid is rapidly becoming a vital instrument of Japanese foreign policy and a sphere in which major changes can be expected.

The reason why the aid programme is so important is that Japan's scope for the development of independent foreign policy is in other ways rather limited. Although Japan nowadays has a sizeable army, navy and air force grouped together under the heading of the Self Defence Forces it is still debarred by its constitution and by popular prejudice from making any use of these forces outside its own frontiers. It is, nevertheless vitally concerned with the security of South-east Asia, not only because of the importance to Japanese exporters of Asian markets, but also because the region straddles the all-important shipping route from Japan to Europe and the Middle East.

If Japanese forces cannot be used to keep the peace in South-east Asia, Japan can still make an economic contribution to the stability of the area—and this, so Foreign Ministry officials argue, is where the aid programme comes in.

Given the indisputable importance of South-east Asia (it is estimated that by 1980 some 600 million tons of oil a year will be passing through the Straits of Malacca on its way to Japan) it is perhaps surprising that the concentration of the aid programme on this part of the world is not even greater than it is. At present official Japanese aid is divided between South-east Asia and what the Japanese call East Asia (South Korea, Formosa, etc.) in a ratio of about six to four while, if private loans and grants are included, the emphasis is about even. The recent pattern of aid commitments as opposed to actual disbursements makes it clear however that in future South-east Asia is going to get a progressively larger share of the available funds, and this impression is confirmed by some of the recent initiatives taken by Japanese politicians.

Shortly before he resigned as Foreign Minister to contest the leadership of the Liberal Democrat party in 1968, Mr Takeo Miki launched the idea of a 1,000 m dollars (£417 m) rehabilitation fund for Vietnam to be put into operation immediately after the end of the war. His idea has been taken up within the Foreign Ministry which is working on the basis of a 200 m dollar (£83 m) programme during the first two postwar years (not all of it, naturally to be contributed by Japan).

Other ventures in regional aid in which Japan has taken prominent parts include the Asian Development Bank (ADB) to which Japan, jointly with the United

States, made the biggest contribution, and the Private Investment Company for Asia (PICA). PICA, like the earlier ADELA (the Atlantic Community Development Group for Latin America) is an organisation devoted to channelling private funds from the developed world into the equity of private companies in developing countries. Its shareholders include leading companies in the United States, Britain, Australasia, and Europe as well as Japan, but it would probably not have come into existence without the efforts of Mr Yoshizane Iwasa, the internationally-minded Chairman of the Fuji Bank, who is also PICA's Chairman.

Japan also initiated the annual Ministerial Meeting for the Economic Development of South-east Asia which held its first session in 1966 and is attended by Malaysia, Singapore, the Philippines, Indonesia, Thailand, Cambodia and Laos as well as Japan itself. The ministerial meeting is officially a forum for the discussion of technical and economic cooperation between the member countries. In practice it also provides a meeting place at which informal negotiations can be held on Japanese bilateral aid to the region.

The total value of Japan's aid in 1968 was 1,049 m dollars (£437 m), an increase of 23 per cent on the previous year and enough to place Japan fourth on the list of donor countries in the DAC (the Development Aid Committee of the Organisation for Economic Cooperation and Development) after the US, France and Germany. As a result of this expansion, Japan moved a step nearer the UN target according to which aid should amount to 1 per cent of the donor country's Gross National Product (the actual Japanese percentage in 1968 was 0·74). But in other respects the programme still fell short of the standards set by some other aid-giving nations. An important part of total outgoings consisted of commercial export credits for periods of over one year (there was a 50 per cent increase in this category of loan) while official aid remained relatively static.

Within the official sector loans at relatively high rates of interest continued to predominate over grants and technical aid remained a much smaller proportion of total outgoings than the average for other DAC countries. A particularly controversial aspect of the aid figures has been the inclusion in some recent years of Japanese shipping credits to flag of convenience countries such as Panama and Liberia, despite the fact that credits of this type have a rather limited relevance to the development of the countries concerned.

Taxed with weaknesses such as these most Japanese officials tend to produce two lines of defence. One is that the official tally of Japanese aid contains some surprising omissions as well as some surprising inclusions. A significant example is the 100 m dollars (£42 m) made available annually to US administered Okinawa, which cannot be included in the programme because to do so would be to undermine the validity of Japan's claim to the island. The other line of defence is that while the weaknesses are present they are being steadily eliminated.

Official aid commitments made in 1968 by Japan showed a major increase in those of the previous year, but were not reflected in the disbursement figures because of administrative delays, many of them in the recipient countries. Interest rates, it is agreed, are still at an undesirably high level, but steps are being taken to combat this problem. One such measure was the passage of legislation redefining the scope of the Overseas Economic Cooperation Fund, the Japanese Government's self-loan agency which was previously unable to deal with anything but orthodox development projects.

The OECF is entitled by its amended charter to promote 'stability' as well as 'development' in recipient countries, a change which means that it could for example lend money to particularly hard-pressed countries such as Indonesia for the financing of basic commodity imports.

The reform which many Japanese aid officials would most like to see is the establishment of a separate agency to handle aid on the lines of either Britain's Overseas Development Ministry, or the US Agency for International Development, or perhaps with features drawn from both. Most of the administration of the Japanese aid programme is at present done by the 100 or so senior staff members of the Foreign Ministry's Economic Cooperation Bureau who rightly regard themselves as being overloaded, but the Finance Ministry and the Ministry of International Trade and Industry both maintain a close watch on the details as well as the general shape of the programme and would be unwilling to relax their controls.

The establishment of a separate agency—especially one subject to the overall direction of the Foreign Ministry—might well be seen as a challenge to the authority of the Finance Ministry, the most powerful as well as the most prestigious organ of the Japanese Government, and for that reason the move may be slow in coming. This does not alter the fact that it is probably inevitable, given the rapidly growing importance of aid as an instrument of Japan's foreign policy.

27

Defence

Japan is rather more than halfway through the implementation of her third five-year defence plan (1967–71). This involves the creation of a defensive, non-nuclear missile system covering the whole archipelago from Wakkanai to Kagoshima, and it has meant some increase in the numbers of the Ground Self Defence Force (now approaching 200,000) as well as the strengthening of the Maritime and Air Self Defence Forces.

There has been an important change in the public attitude to the armed services. An opinion poll by *Asahi Shimbun* at the end of 1968 revealed the interesting fact that nearly 65 per cent of those interviewed believed that the nation ought to have its own defence forces. Until quite recently it would have been difficult to find much support for rearmament of any kind. The same *Asahi* poll, it is worth noting, showed that 21 per cent would not oppose Japanese possession of nuclear weapons.

All the same, the use of force to back diplomacy is still generally regarded in Japan as immoral and unwise. It is seen as permissible only in dire circumstances, such as an actual invasion of the Japanese homeland. And if the Self Defence Forces are no longer looked upon as pariahs they have yet to be invested with genuinely popular appeal. The head of state, the Emperor, continues to have no relationship, formal or otherwise, with the armed services of his country. This state of affairs, so different from the situation a generation ago, is illustrated by the oath taken by those who enlist in the Defence Forces. The recruit swears that he 'will fight to the death in defence of the Japanese race'. In his commitment to his duties as a serviceman there is no reference to the historic imperial house. The armed forces, then, are accepted as a fact of life; and most people in Japan, despite the clause in the constitution forbidding the existence of such forces, seem ready to concede that national defence has become an obligation that cannot be evaded.

It is an obligation that vitally affects Japanese-American relations. The Foreign Minister has spoken of the need to maintain 'the security arrangements with the United States' (the US-Japan Security Pact) in order 'to supplement the deficiency' in Japan's capacity to defend herself. What 'deficiency' in particular did the Foreign Minister have in mind? One guesses that what was meant was the nuclear deterrent. Since nuclear testing and stockpiling by Japan would be political suicide at the moment—the Government is committed to the three principles of the non-manufacture, non-possession and non-introduction of nuclear weapons—and since the American nuclear deterrent, according to orthodox doctrine, is the ultimate guarantee of Japan's security, it follows that the Security Pact must remain in force, whatever minor revisions and adjustments are made. The socialists may look at things very differently; but from the point of view of the ruling Liberal-Democratic party the possibility that Washington, thanks to Vietnam, may have to reshape American policy in Asia makes it the more imperative that the Security Pact should not be placed in jeopardy.

But this is where the Okinawa problem comes in. There is a general expectation that Okinawa will be returned to Japanese rule either in 1970 or within, at most, two years from that date. Before this happens the United States can use its bases on Okinawa to implement policies throughout the Far East. But once Okinawa reverts to Japanese jurisdiction the American bases on the island will have to operate on lines similar to those that apply to American bases in Japan. Such is the firm conviction, it seems, of the Japanese. In other words, American forces in Okinawa will be welcome only in so far as they are seen to exist purely for the defence of Japan. The majority of the Japanese people, it is fair to say, are not interested in—and may indeed be hostile towards—American plans and policies outside the orbit of the Japanese islands.

Thus it is extremely unlikely, whatever pressure may be exerted by Washington, that Japan will join a regional defence pact covering any part of South-east Asia. No doubt the Maritime Self-Defence Force may feel it could fulfil a useful role in future, should need arise, by helping to keep open the Malacca Strait, on Japan's economic lifeline to the oil wells of the Middle East. Ideas of this kind will have a wider circulation in Japan if it becomes clear that all British forces are to be withdrawn from South-east Asia. Yet the probability remains that the Japanese Government will be most cautious. Indeed, the defence of South-east Asia, in which the Japanese Maritime Force could play a valuable part, is something to which no Government in Tokyo could be officially committed during the 1970s.

There is also the question of Korea. Can this peninsula, geographically so close to Japan, be regarded as being outside the orbit of the Japanese islands? In a famous Press conference early in 1950 Secretary of State Acheson implied that Korea was outside the orbit; and it has been claimed that this was a factor in North Korea's decision to attack the South. Consequently there is no doubt that since 1950 American strategists have recognised that Japan's frontier is on the 38th Parallel. Do Japanese defence planners see the situation in the same light?

During the past year the activities of Communist guerrillas in South Korea have increased to an alarming degree. Moreover, there is evidently a good deal of agitation and unrest not necessarily provoked by the extreme Left. Faced with these problems, President Park's regime in Seoul has been inclined to adopt an uncompromising stance, bearing down harshly on all dissent and opposition, interpreting these as little short of treason. Yet on one issue all Koreans are united. They are determined that never again will they allow themselves to accept political guidance from Japan. Therefore, no Japanese in a position of official responsibility dare admit in public that Japan is vitally interested in what happens in Korea. But the fact is that the Japanese, whether they like it or not, must be concerned very profoundly with what goes on in Korea. In this sense the 38th Parallel is indeed part of Japan's national frontier. Thus if one can imagine the Self Defence Forces operating anywhere outside the homeland during the 1970s it is only in the context of Korea—in the air over Korea and in Korean waters— that such a scenario is conceivable. And only the gravest emergency, such as successful armed aggression by the North, could bring matters to this pass.

Lion Dance at Hida, Honshu.

28

The leisure boom

Leaving aside a small minority who, through sickness or other misfortune or sheer bad luck, have missed the bus, the entire Japanese people may be said to share to the full in Japan's national prosperity. But it would be wrong to imply that everyone in Japan is rolling in money. Rich people in Japan—and there are quite a number of them nowadays—do not go in for conspicuous spending. No luxury yachts, no weekend estates. On the other hand there is plenty of money about. One sees evidence of it in the crowded department stores and in the lavish entertaining that goes on in the luxury hotels. But most Japanese families would no doubt say that they are not finding it easy to make both ends meet. They would complain about the rising cost of living and say that they could do with more money. Nonetheless, the nation is well fed, well dressed, and well equipped with the appurtenances of our age. There is hardly a family without a television set or washing machine, and many have a refrigerator and a host of other gadgets. Eggs, bread, milk, chicken and pork supplement the traditional diet of rice, fish, vegetables and bean paste soup, and account for 20 per cent of the family budget as compared with 10 per cent in 1955.

Department stores flourish and carry a wide range of

inexpensive clothing in all the latest styles, so that people (and especially children) in outlying districts are no less smartly turned out than those in Tokyo. And there is money left over after these necessities are taken care of to spend on entertainment and travel. This is usually referred to in Japan as the 'leisure boom'. Though work dominates everyday life, numerous pleasures can now be enjoyed by all—some undreamed of by the previous generation, though they are essentially pleasures performed *en masse*. Golf is for the rich, or at least for the higher echelons of businessmen; but ski-ing, hiking, swimming, mountain climbing and many other active and passive leisure-time activities are available for all. As anyone who has visited Japan in recent years will testify, the Japanese are dedicated travellers. In 1968 17 million people visited the Hakone National Park, and at weekends in the summer millions flock to the beaches. Sightseeing buses carried over 200 million eager tourists to the four corners of the Japanese islands in 1967. One person in twenty-four now owns a motor car and the ratio is decreasing rapidly. In the home there is television, which is now one of the main features of Japanese life. If you reside in the Tokyo area you have a choice of six channels all going from 6.30 in the morning until midnight and all showing some programmes in colour. Early morning shows claim some of the biggest audiences. One daily show which starts at 7.30 a.m. has a nationwide audience of about 24 million, while another station with a rival show starting a bit later enjoys similar popularity. But having said all this, it must be conceded that the quality of life for most people in Japan still leaves much to be desired—notably in the matter of housing which lags behind badly, but also in such matters as public hygiene, medical services, and roads.

The rapid transition from traditional austerity to near-affluence has brought with it a number of new problems. Some of these are common to all the developed countries with high living standards. For example, congested highways, horrifying road accident statistics, air pollution, noise, and the disposal of an ever-increasing quantity of almost indestructible refuse. But the special problems which prosperity has brought to Japan stem mainly from the fact that 100 million people have to exist in a small and limited land area, compounded by the rapid urbanisation of the population during the past fifteen years. Its effect on the social fabric has been profound. Twenty years ago, more than 50 per cent of the working population lived on the land. Today the figure is about 19 per cent, and the drift away from the land continues.

Every year at the end of March (the graduation season) tens of thousands of youngsters who have graduated from middle school or high school pour in from the country to the urban industrial centres where labour-hungry industry is waiting to absorb them. It is this increasing urbanisation which makes the housing problem in the cities so difficult to solve. Few urban families in Japan have more than two rooms and many have to exist in only one room. Living in one room in Japanese style is not quite as bad as it may sound because the room is not cluttered with bedsteads and chairs and so on; but still it scarcely makes for gracious living. Every young married couple longs for a house of their own with a garden, but it is very unlikely that many of them can ever realise it.

The high population density in most of Japan affects every aspect of life. In particular it imposes a terrifying degree of conformity on people, regardless of their station in the community. In a society dedicated to the idea of fair shares for all and where pressure on land and resources is so intense, there is really little scope for individual flamboyance or even for the exercise of individual preference except in minor matters. This need to conform is perhaps more readily accepted by the Japanese people, with their long experience of a closely regulated society under the Tokugawa Shogunate, than it would be by other nations. In a nation of 100 million in a territory where more than 80 per cent of the land is inhospitable mountain, restrictions on individual freedom of action are inescapable to avoid the situation of a free-for-all and the devil take the hindmost.

At all events, although nearly everybody is better off financially than ever before, life for most people in today's affluent Japan is fairly circumscribed and tends to follow a set pattern which varies remarkably little between one individual and another. Education is free, and almost without exception everyone attends a state school whose curriculum is laid down by the Ministry of Education. A proportion, perhaps 20 to 30 per cent, leave at the end of their middle school course when they are fourteen or fifteen. A further 30 per cent or so leave on graduating from High School at seventeen or eighteen. The remainder go on to a university or technical college.

The aim of most young men is to enter the employment of a modern industrial company and those who do so can see their future precisely mapped out for them. The new entrant does not expect to change his job throughout his working life. He knows that for the first ten years he will be expected to work long hours for comparatively little reward. After that, if all goes well, he can expect promotion at intervals, first deputy section chief, then to section chief, next to deputy head of a department and so on up the scale. At each step upward he will become eligible not only for a bigger salary but also for the improved fringe benefits that go with the higher position: a better house or apartment, increased allowances for entertainment, membership of a golf club, and eventually the allotment to him for his personal use of a car and chauffeur. If he runs true to pattern he will not look for hobbies or pursuits outside his work and will find complete satisfaction in the diversions which his job affords. At a certain age he retires and then qualifies for a fairly substantial gratuity. But *not* a pension. Until recently the retirement age was fifty-five, but because of the shortage of labour there is a move in some quarters to raise it to fifty-eight and even to sixty. It is all very cut and dried and with only minor variations the same for people in all walks of life.

This pattern of existence seems to have satisfied most people's aspirations until very recently. But there are signs that the younger people now moving up in the business hierarchy may in the future look for something more adventurous and rewarding and less like a blueprint. It is not easy to foresee an improvement in this direction, however, because the pressure on resources and living-space is likely to increase rather than diminish. Japan now ranks twentieth in the world league tables in terms of *per capita* income; but only recently a responsible member of a prominent firm of American consultants expressed the view that by the end of the century the Japanese *per capita* income could conceivably overtake that of the United States. If this, or anything approaching it, comes about there will be enormous surplus wealth in individual hands to be soaked up. One possibility—hardly yet discussed publicly in Japan—is that with the rapid advance of technology, much greater use might be made of the hitherto unused land area. If only one-tenth of this could be reclaimed for human habitation or other practical use it could transform the prospects for the Japanese people.

Beyond this, massive capital investment will be required in the public sector before the real standard of living of the Japanese people approaches that of West Europe. Despite the modern highways that have been built, and others under construction, the road system as a whole is inadequate and more than four-fifths of the roads remain unsurfaced. Sewerage systems are all but non-existent. Only about a third of Tokyo, the largest city in the world, with a population of nearly 12 million, for example, has sewers, and the situation in the other large cities is no better. The medical facilities, particularly in rural areas, are poor and many more hospitals are needed.

It is in these directions rather than in actively seeking a major world role that the Japanese are likely to turn their formidable energies and wealth in the next decade or so. The determination to achieve equality of status with the West has been the consistent driving force behind Japan's advance ever since 1868, the year of the Meiji restoration. It was this ambition indeed which led to the disaster of the last war. In international terms the goal of equal status has at last been attained, but the Japanese people will not be satisfied until their personal standard of living is fully equal to that of the West.

The question which most disturbs thinking people in Japan today is the deep division between the young and old. This phenomenon is one which affects all the developed countries, not excluding those of the Communist bloc, but the division seems deeper in Japan than elsewhere. The young people of today, those below the age of about twenty-five or thirty, are very different from their parents at the same age, and many Japanese are bewildered by their children's behaviour. These young people with their irreverent views in fact do not behave in the accepted Japanese way at all—to the old-fashioned members of Japanese society they are more like foreigners than Japanese. Their sense of values seems utterly different from that of the older generation, which regarded frugality and austerity as among the greatest virtues and held in high esteem such things as unswerving loyalty, obedience to authority, and diligence. All these, except possibly the last, the new generation appears to have thrown out of the window as meaningless trappings of a feudalistic past.

It is, however, a matter of observation that in Japan as young people get older they tend to revert to traditional ways. For instance, a Japanese newspaper which conducted an investigation into the present whereabouts of the unruly student leaders who helped organise the near-riots over the Security Treaty in 1960 which led to the fall of the then Prime Minister and the cancellation of the visit of President Eisenhower discovered that the great majority of them, now in their middle thirties, had settled down in conventional jobs as business executives and were busy raising families of their own. Even 'Westernised' men of a certain comfortable income group after middle age seem to find pleasure in purely Japanese pursuits like the tea ceremony, composing Japanese poetry, and tending rock gardens or dwarf plants, attired in the native kimono. And there is certainly no doubt that most of the younger people are hard workers. Dr Herman Kahn, an American politico-economist and a noted seer, caused quite a stir in Japan with a statement about a year or two ago in which he is reported to have said that if the nineteenth century was Britain's century, the twentieth century was America's; and the twenty-first century would be Japan's, provided—and this is the point—provided the Japanese continued to be as industrious as they are now.

29

Visual arts

It is little more than a century since Japanese art was first brought to the notice of the occidental world to any appreciable extent. The earliest exhibition of Japanese art in London was staged in 1854 and seems to have excited little interest at the time. After the Meiji restoration, however, Japanese art became increasingly familiar in the West and, by the 1880s, resulted in a craze for anything and everything Japanese. The arts of Japan exerted a curious influence on the applied and decorative arts of Europe and America in the closing decades of the nineteenth century, which manifested itself in such diverse fields as bamboo furniture and the *Art Nouveau* glass of Louis Tiffany.

Yet Western exposure to the art of Japan was nothing new. Ever since the ships of the Honourable East India Company and its Dutch and Portuguese counterparts had penetrated to the Far East at the end of the sixteenth century Japanese lacquered furniture and the porcelain of Arita had been exported to Europe. Unfortunately this contact with the outside world was comparatively shortlived, and during the long period of the Tokugawa shogunate (1615–1868) Japan was cut off culturally and aesthetically, as well as commercially, from Europe and even the rest of Asia. It is a matter for conjecture how far the rapid developments in Western art which took place in that period might have affected the art of Japan.

The only influences on Japan at that time emanated from China or Korea and the fact that they were copied enthusiastically and given a distinctive Japanese character indicates something of the imagination and artistic feeling of the Japanese. When Japanese art, in the form of porcelain, ivory carvings or prints, was first introduced to the West in the mid-nineteenth century it was hailed for its refreshing novelty and originality. Somewhat later, however, Chinese art was similarly introduced to the West and a reaction against Japanese art set in, a popular, if oversimplified, feeling being that Japan had merely imitated the older culture. This assessment was grossly inaccurate, overlooking the very real and often unique contributions of Japanese art in every medium, adding many new elements and in some respects even surpassing the art of the older Chinese culture.

A fundamental point about Japanese art is that the arts and crafts have always been inextricably linked. Even the most mundane crafts were exalted to the status of an art and such diverse occupations as flower arranging and calligraphy have long been imbued with an artistry which few other nations would have thought worth bringing to bear on them. To the Japanese all art is one and art is all-pervading. Thus although the Japanese have borrowed or assimilated much in recent years from the arts of other countries, their innate good taste has invested this with a distinctly Japanese character. Even the Post-Impressionist paintings of Foujita (who spent many years in France) are typically Japanese in style, though a good many of his ideas on colour and representation were derived from the French school.

The World War II was responsible for both the neglect and the increased popularity of Japanese art in other parts of the world. The political unpopularity of Japan before and during the war militated against an unprejudiced appreciation of Japanese art, while the closer contact with the West, arising primarily out of the American occupation of Japan at the end of the war, has led to an astonishing increase in interest in Japanese art in general. Thirty years ago Japanese art, apart from a few well-known reproductions of Hokusai prints, was virtually the closed preserve of the scholar and orientalist; now wood and ivory carving, pottery and porcelain, lacquer-ware and prints, sword-fittings and textiles are collected and studied by countless thousands, and the rate at which interest in Japanese art has grown in the past two years alone has been truly phenomenal. Inevitably this has had a marked

The Great Wave at Kanazawa: one of thirty Views of Mount Fuji *by Hokusai.*

upward effect on prices of even the humblest piece of *tsuba* or the most insignificant *netsuke*. In the auction season of 1967–68, for example, Sotheby's held sixteen sales devoted to Japanese works of art, totalling £208,368; in the season of 1968–69 fifteen sales resulted in a grand total of £375,195—an impressive increase in which all previous records for Japanese works of art were broken.

Paintings and prints

Paradoxically it was the insular period of the Tokugawa shogunate which gave to the world Japan's greatest contribution to art, the colour print. The complete isolation of Japan from the outside world and the intellectual stagnation which was its concomitant was strangely paralleled in the rise of a powerful and prosperous bourgeoisie. About 1615 the Tokugawa Ieyasu transferred his capital from Kyoto to the village of Edo which grew rapidly into what is now the most populous city in the world—Tokyo. The merchant classes of Edo waxed rich at the expense of the peasantry and the samurai alike and by the end of the seventeenth century had emerged not only as the real economic power in Japan but also as patrons of new forms in art, which broke away from the classical traditions. It was in this atmosphere that the Sotatsu-Korin school of art flourished characterised by the bold use of colour and a highly unorthodox approach to perspective which is both captivating and endearing. Sotatsu, who flourished in the early years of the Edo period, experimented with new techniques based on old concepts, but his distant relative, Ogata Korin, perfected the decorative style as shown in his screen paintings of flowers. Many of the artists of the ensuing century were also poets and they habitually decorated their pictures with lines of poetry. To the uninitiated these *haikus* may appear to have been added artlessly to fill an otherwise empty space, but the casual appearance of this calligraphy is deceptive; it would be as carefully thought out and deliberately executed as the brushwork of the picture itself.

In contrast with the bold experimentalism of the Sotatsu-Korin school was the stiff, formalised painting of the Kano school, official painters to the shoguns. The vast Kano clan, comprising numerous families related to one another and all engaged in painting, provided the bulk of the material required by the Japanese ruling classes in the seventeenth and eighteenth centuries. These two streams of painting, catering on the one hand to the *nouveaux riches* and on the other to the more conservative samurai, ran parallel throughout Japanese art right down to the time of the Restoration in 1868. In the Meiji period, which saw the floodgates of Western culture opened on an unsuspecting Japan, traditional painting, as so much in Japanese art, was weakened, but still remained vigorous. During the present century traditional painting has revived.

Oddly enough, although the Japanese developed the art of print-making to a high degree of perfection the very cheapness of these colour prints made them despised and neglected by art connoisseurs in the country of their origin. Broadly speaking, the colour print of the seventeenth century was evolved for a mass market, but one of the most hypercritical and discriminating markets in the world. The poorer urban classes, who could not aspire to own a Sotatsu, far less a Kano, original, settled quite happily for a print by Moronobu or his successors. Before about 1740 these prints were produced in black and white and had to be coloured by hand, but between that date and 1764 printers evolved the technique of the multicolour print. The *nishi-ke*, or 'brocade paintings', often required up to ten different blocks; the intricate cutting and imposition of these blocks in perfect register was a task requiring the most exacting skill and patience. These technical developments came at a time when some of the greatest masters of the Japanese print were at work. Among them Harunobu and Utamaro have attained international fame for their mastery of the print. In the early nineteenth century they were succeeded by the equally famous Hokusai and Hiroshige, both of whom were exceptionally prolific in their output. Countless thousands of their prints were produced,

An ivory of Shou Loo, the god of Longevity; a wooden netsuke showing a monkey and a tortoise.

many of them finding their way to the West in the 1880s and helping to stimulate interest in Japanese art in general.

Pottery and porcelain

Pottery has been produced in Japan from the very earliest times, the elaborate Tea Ceremony giving special meaning and impetus to the manufacture of *chawan* and *chaire*, the bowls, cups and utensils involved in this ritual. The influence of the Tea Ceremony on the development of Japanese culture cannot be over-estimated. In ceramics, in particular, it probably arrested the development of porcelain, which was not produced in Japan till the early seventeenth century, and accounts for the fact that pottery, rather than porcelain, is more highly regarded in Japan even today. By contrast Japanese pottery is little understood or collected in the West, and conversely, while Japanese porcelain has long been popular in Europe and America, it is only in recent years that it has begun to receive the serious attention of collectors in Japan itself.

The introduction of an indigenous porcelain industry to Japan was due to Korean immigrants working in the Kutani district in the early decades of the seventeenth century. The true Kutani wares were outstanding for their subtle use of dark hues of purple and green against a deep yellow background. The output of the Kutani factory was relatively small and little of the better material ever left the country. Unfortunately for the reputation of Kutani, numerous copies of this attractive porcelain were produced in the nineteenth and twentieth centuries and most of the so-called Kutani ware now in even the most respectable collections outside Japan are no more than imitations produced at Arita long after the original Kutani kilns had ceased production.

The well-deserved reputation of Japanese porcelain rests mainly on the products of the Arita district, the

Kakiemon and Imari enamelled porcelains. Kakiemon was the name of a family of potters who are traditionally credited with having invented the characteristic red overglaze about 1640 (though some authorities are of the opinion that this must have taken place a generation later). The Kakiemon school mastered the techniques and art of the Chinese K'ang-hsi period so thoroughly that their porcelain was exported in vast quantities to China as well as being sent to Europe. Among the many motifs which the Kakiemon potters favoured were the rose, cherry-blossom, prunus, phoenix and deer, but it is in the vigorous use of the enamel overglaze that the style is seen at its most distinctive.

The small town of Imari was the port from which most of the porcelain of Arita, and the surrounding district, was shipped to Nagasaki and thus it has bestowed its name somewhat loosely on a wide range of wares. The most characteristic of the so-called Imari porcelains, however, may be recognised by the combination of underglaze blue, red enamel and gold, to which green, yellow, aubergine, blue and black enamels were often added. A fair amount of Japanese porcelain always succeeded in finding its way, via China and the East Indies, to the European market, but it was after the Restoration of 1868 that this trade assumed gigantic proportions. In recent years porcelain, rather neglected in the land of its origin, has been enjoying a marked reassessment, with the result that much of the better material coming up at auction in Europe and America is being repatriated to meet the new demand.

Netsuke, inro okimono and tsuba

The netsuke of Japan is quite unlike any other art form in the world. Literally it means a toggle (from the verb *tsukeni*, to fasten) but from being a mere dress accessory it developed into a miniature form of sculpture illustrating the folklore, customs and history of Japan.

Netsuke is thought to have existed as early as the fifteenth century when, in the primitive form of pieces of wood or bone, toggles were used to secure a cord to the *obi* (wide sash or belt) from which were suspended a variety of objects, since pockets in the occidental sense were not a feature of the kimonos worn by both sexes.

Under the Tokugawa shogunate ornate carving came to be applied to netsuke and by the middle of the nineteenth century these charming trifles had become popular all over the country and at all levels of society. Netsuke took a great variety of forms, the commonest being human figures, the twelve signs of the zodiac, and masks derived from the *Noh* drama. Wood and ivory were the materials most frequently used, but stones such as coral, amber and jade were occasionally used and bone or narwhal horn are sometimes met with. The use of netsuke declined after 1868 when more and more Japanese forsook the kimono for Western forms of dress. Netsuke was relegated to the souvenir and curio shop, to be purchased by Western tourists. It is only since World War II that netsuke has developed enormously as a subject for serious study and collecting. The prices fetched for fine netsuke in the seven-part sale of the Hindson Collection at Sotheby's in 1968–69 demonstrate the remarkable increase in interest. Before the sale in March 1969 no netsuke had attained a price of 2,400 dollars (£1,000); in that sale one item set a new world record at 4,080 dollars (£1,700). In the final sale, in June 1969, three items actually passed the 4,800 dollar (£2,000) mark.

Often associated with netsuke are *inro*, the ornately carved or lacquered boxes which were suspended from the *obi* and contained medicines, writing materials and other small articles. Most of these intriguing little boxes consisted of several compartments, intricately jointed and decorated, often matching the netsuke in style, design and materials. No account of Japanese carving would be complete without some reference to the *okimono*, small figures carved in wood and, particularly after 1868, in ivory. The decline in the use of netsuke after the Restoration threw many ivory carvers out of work so they turned to the production of exquisite little *okimono* instead, to cater to the growing tourist trade. While a great deal of *okimono* can be dismissed as mere tourist souvenirs, it should be noted that since the foundation of the Tokyo Fine Art School in 1888 the art of ivory carving has been revived and greatly developed.

The other small class of object which is typically Japanese and which has captured the interest of Western collectors in recent years is *tsuba*, the ornamental sword-guards which were a product of the golden age of the samurai. The majority of *tsuba* were worked in iron with contrasting inlays of gold; others were produced in alloys of gold and silver with copper and punched, engraved or incised with a wide range of decoration. As the necessity to bear arms receded *tsuba* became less utilitarian and more extravagantly decorated but this in no way detracts from their aesthetic appeal.

30

The theatre

There are two main traditional forms of Japanese theatre—*Noh* and *Kabuki*. Both are highly stylised and lack the kind of dramatic action that will connect Western audiences with their previous theatrical experience. However, a number of Western writers have been influenced by the refined, almost ascetic, approach of *Noh* drama. This is reflected in the bare stage of many modern plays in the West, and a return to the use of masks on stage.

Many visitors have found that the Japanese theatre is one area where they have felt most estranged from, yet fascinated by, Japanese culture.

Noh drama is the outcome of a synthesis, in the early fifteenth century, of the existing Japanese theatrical tradition. The background of *Noh* drama has its roots in what was known as *sarugaku*, or monkey music. This was a series of acrobatic juggling and comic feats and dances, some of them thought to have originated in ancient China. For several centuries prior to the 1400s, *saragaku* had been placed under the protection of temples: this gave it a refinement and, at the same time, it served to fuse religious precepts.

Noh also draws on other traditions, such as *dengaku*, or rice-field music, which was an ancient harvest rite. *Noh* flourished in the fifteenth and sixteenth centuries and was the principal form of entertainment for the aristocracy. Over 1,000 plays were written of which half are extant and some 200 are actually still in repertory. There is no unity of time, place or action in the play. Instead there is a unity of rhythm and tone; for instance the dialogue is based on phrases of one or seven syllables. The rhythm of action and dialogue is complemented throughout by a drum, the principal element in a four-instrument orchestra. The play's construction embodies this unity of rhythm. The drama opens, after a short music prologue, with the appearance of the *waki*—a secondary character, generally in the guise of a monk—who explains his presence and states where the action is taking place. The principal character —the *shite*—then appears, perhaps in the guise of a farmer, and fills in more background. He then disappears, to return in his guise as hero or principal character. The action is developed through a series of dialogues between him and other secondary characters which are in turn taken up by a chorus. The actors accompany this with mime, slow dance and highly refined movements with, for instance, fans. The themes are classified into five main groups—such as ghosts and warriors, love and demons and goblins. *Noh* drama requires great feats from the actors, who have spent many years in training. There is also constant and imaginative use of masks, some of which are extremely old and have been passed down through generations of actors.

After the sixteenth century *Noh* ceased to be written but its acting traditions continued. Originally the plays were performed outside and on temporary stages. The present day stage is very simple with a small square platform and four pillars supporting a roof. The wings are connected by a gangway. The stage is thus open on three sides. The impression of simplicity is increased by the lack of decor—just a pine tree painted on the backdrop—and an almost total absence of props. Each *Noh* play lasts roughly one hour; but the plays are usually presented as programmes arranged along the following traditional lines: first a sacred play, then a heroic battle story followed by a feminine play, a fantastic play and then a terminal play (sometimes with a love theme). An extra piece can be included for ceremonial occasions.

There are four main schools of *Noh* drama: *Kanze*, *Komparu*, *Kongo* and *Hosho*. Three theatres in Tokyo show *Noh* plays: Kanze-Kaikan, Hoshokai and Kita.

Kabuki

Whereas *Noh* drama was a courtly amusement and now mainly appeals to intellectuals, *Kabuki* is and always has been popular entertainment. This is emphasised in

The Hero in a Kabuki play impersonates a samurai.

the way that a *Kabuki* theatre has a special actors' gangway to the stage which traverses the auditorium, while a *Noh* audience is separated from the actors by a gravel space.

Kabuki originated in Kyoto in the early 1600s where dancers began to elaborate on sung religious pantomime. Gradually narrative was included. *Kabuki* proper really began after 1631 when men took over the female parts, a tradition still followed. The chief roles of a *Kabuki* actor are: *Tachi Yaku*, the male lead; *Kataki Yaku*, the traitor; *Onnagata,* the female lead; *Kasha,* the old woman; *Wakashu*, the young cavalier; and *Doke*, the clown. These characters are woven into favourite themes of combat, vengeance, love and ghost stories concerning popular or legendary figures. Although they can be contemporary, more often than not they are drawn from Japan's feudal history from the twelfth to the sixteenth centuries.

The actors have to be extremely versatile and they take years to learn their characters' gestures. They tend to take the audience by storm, not hesitating to scream and shout or carry out gruesome actions on stage. *Kabuki* is a vehicle for actors and not writers, although adaptations via *Kabuki* have been made of Western plays.

In 1888 an attempt was made to adapt *Kabuki* to contemporary conditions. For the first time women were allowed to play female roles and certain aspects of the Western theatre were added. This breakaway group came to be known as the *Shimpa* Theatre.

In contrast to *Noh, Kabuki* generally has decor, while its stage is much larger and longer. The stage is also fitted out with a revolving platform and a trapdoor. Watching *Kabuki* can take as long as eight hours for a full programme. In Tokyo there are usually two sessions a day at some four theatres (11.00 to 15.30; 16.30 to 22.00). The Tokyo *kabuki* theatres are: Kabuki-Za (most used to catering for foreigners and has programmes in English); the National Theatre; Shin-

bashi-Embujo and Meiji-Za. As Kyoto is the traditional home of *Kabuki*, performances are also staged
there.

Bunraku

Bunraku is drama using puppets, from a third to a sixth
of life size. Although it is slowly dying as an art, performances are still given at certain times of the year at
Osaka, where it originated in the seventeenth century.
It developed from the courtly *joruri* ballads which
recounted stories equivalent to those of the European
troubadours. The performance is carried out with the
puppet operator visible on stage (a miniature reproduc-
tion of the *Kabuki* theatre), helped by two assistants.
A chanter and a *samisen* (three-stringed guitar) accompany the play. The Asahi-Za Theatre at Osaka is
traditionally the home of the *Bunraku*.

31

Films

The Japanese film has a good reputation overseas, and has done more to 'explain' Japan to the outside world than most Japanese realise. Certain Japanese films have become classics, and half a dozen directors have acquired international reputations. Outside Europe and America only the Indians and the Japanese have produced a long succession of good and successful films. For the latter it is a very special achievement, given the extent to which Japan has been isolated from the rest of the world—the film still communicates, while the Japanese linguistic barrier remains Himalayan.

It was not until after World War II that the Japanese film became known overseas. There had been a large and flourishing industry during the 1920s and 1930s, but it had no standing internationally. Japanese would go to Hollywood for a year or two and return to their country with pronounced ideas as to how to run their own shows. But the reverse flow was negligible. Part of the reason for this exceptional isolation may have been the odd nature of the Japanese production companies. They were very Japanese and inward-looking. Films were not made for export: silk goods and cotton cloth were.

The production companies—Nikkatsu, Shockiku, Toho, for example—were extremely busy churning out feature films at a great rate. But they had rather crabbed notions about the outside world. This was still apparent after the war right up and until the point where the Japanese film had its first major success overseas—with *Rashomon*. This famous psychological tale of rape (or was it passion?) was submitted to a Venice jury in 1951 in a most absent-minded manner. Its triumph surprised the producer, Daiei. Thereafter, the Japanese film went from strength to strength overseas, in artistic reputation. At home the industry consolidated.

The Japanese film industry was never so prosperous as in the late 1950s. Television was still just around the corner, and the big producers—Nikkatsu, Shochiku and Toho had been joined by Daiei and Toei—had split the domestic market between them in a classic 'oligopolistic' manner, while agreeing not to steal each other's stars. The output of the industry was high, with each big company trying to finish at least one feature film a week. It was a rush, but it worked. From time to time one of the leading directors would be given free rein. It was in this period that such films as the *Seven Samurai*, *Ikiru* and *Tokyo Story* were completed. While the nation was struggling to get back on its feet in economic terms, the film industry was showing its maturity.

Television, the newcomer, had as serious an impact on the film industry in Japan as anywhere else in the world. In the 1960s the financial picture changed rapidly, as it had often done before in the Japanese film industry. One company—the oldest of the big firms, Nikkatsu—sank deep into the red. The decline did not affect everyone equally. Toho, with its hands firmly on the urban market, and Toei, the vigorous newcomer of the 1950s which would touch any kind of film, without preconceptions, held up better than the others.

Along with the commercial problems went a general decline in artistic standards. The industry had become more conservative, if possible, and less willing to give opportunities to good directors. The 1960s has not seen a long stream of commercial and artistic success comparable to the 1950s in Japan. Productions became heavier in style, safer in content, and played to tied houses in the big cities with most success. It was a platform built for Toho, and the company did not miss its opportunity. The success of Toho outweighed that of all other production companies by a very long way. In the last full year for which records are available (fiscal 1967) Toho scored six out of the top seven films. The most successful Japanese film in that year was *The Sun of Kurobe,* a 'nice' family film about building dams, which netted 796 m yen (over £900,000 or 2.2 m dollars) according to one estimate. The film was made by Nikkatsu, but the next six most popular films were all Toho productions. Three of them were comedies, a fourth was a vehicle for the Japanese star Yuzo Kayama and there was also a *chambara* (sword-fighting) special.

Toho's most successful production in that year was *The Longest Day,* a blow-by-blow account of the last days before the Pacific war ended. This film was unique in showing the Japanese Emperor on the screen for the first time—though the Emperor was seen in profile. It was also the only one of the ten most financially successful films to be liked by Japanese critics.

There has been a parting of the ways, for while the big producers continue with their average works, the better quality films are almost all being made by small independents. It is the old story of commercialism in the film industry. Much talent remains in the big production companies, but it usually gets ironed out in the studios. The bigger productions lack flavour; the independents, on the other hand, work slowly and take greater care in preparation. Above all they exercise discrimination.

The best independent productions display political attitudes of which Toho, for example, may be declared innocent. Whether they are set in feudal times (the Samurai-servant relationship) or in modern industrial Japan (bad treatment of workers by 'feudal' bosses)

187

they say something about Japan which the big producers do not aspire to do: they criticise their own bottled-up society, its politics and its sex—frank treatment of sexual themes is hardly to be expected from any but the independents, despite the Japanese cinema's reputation for erotic and sadistic delights.

This reputation has been more or less well maintained by the independents in 1969 in Japan—the film becoming if anything more tortured, more gory and, naturally, more sexy. The Japanese film has inevitably followed the international trend. There is much removing of clothes, heaving of shoulders and ambivalent embracing. Homosexual themes are being pursued more vigorously than ever, as in *Bara No Soretsu*, by Matsumoto, in which there are long naked love scenes. The film closes with the sixteen-year-old hero/heroine poking out his eyes with a knife—a scene in which the audience is spared very little.

However, blood rather than sex remains the more reliable commercial ingredient for the big companies. There has been another wave of *chambara* (swordfighting) movies in 1969, the most successful of which have been made by the big companies. Toho is said to have netted 600 m yen (1.7 m dollars or £700,000) and 400 m yen (1.1 m dollars or £450,000) respectively from its best *Chambara* films this year. Daiei followed through with *Hitogiri,* another *chambara* delight starring leading novelist, Yukio Michima. There is a tremendous amount of gore in *Hitogiri*, so much so that Mishima's favoured *hara-kiri* scene passes almost quietly.

The maxim that blood sells better than sex holds true only in the middle and upper reaches of the film industry. At the base of the pyramid, in the flea-pits, the 'pink' movie houses, and the most basic big city cinemas, all linked with independent producers, it is sex all the way. This is the market for the 'eroduction' (Japanese-English for 'erotic production'), and what a market it is. Half of the 400 to 500 films made every year in Japan are eroductions, strung together on tiny budgets with out-of-work actors and actresses—and said to cover their costs in the first week of showing.

The eroduction is an indelicate 'quicky' product, strictly sixty minutes long with approximately one copulation every five minutes. It plays on a triple bill with two of its fellows to exclusively male audiences in roughly one third of Japan's cinemas. These films cannot be shown on TV, and the eroduction makers have a firm grip on their market as a result. The profits are,

Shooting a samurai film.

technically, split in a manner unfair to the producer (who takes only 6 per cent). In fact the producer–distributor–cinema-owner chain is a tight one, though, and such a division is often not necessary.

The Japanese film industry is large, sprawling and diffuse yet it should develop in a certain direction. The big producing companies will become more commercial while diversifying well outside an industry with limited growth prospects. This diversification has already gone a long way—few big companies have more than about 60 per cent of their business in films today. The rest is in bowling alleys, taxi firms, hotels and other leisure industry investments. The independents, besides churning out eroductions, will continue to produce most of the artistic films.

32

Entertainments

The geisha

Although in most Western minds the *geisha* is synonymous with Japanese pleasure, the legend far outweighs
the reality. First, there are very few really accomplished
geishas—fewer than 100 in the top class. Second, and
perhaps more important, they cannot be compared with
the Japanese *hosutessu* or hostess. Whereas the hostess
is intended to appeal to simple and well-defined needs,
the *geisha* is both more virtuous and more sophisticated.
Indeed she was originally intended to play the role of a
highly polished entertainer: the ideal of feminine charm,
trained for many years in the art of entertaining men.

In the past *geishas* have often played an important
part in political and social life. Now, they appear
chiefly at banquets, and this is where the businessman
is most likely to see a *geisha*. If a visitor happens to be
a guest at a banquet and a *geisha* performs, it is not out
of place for the visitor to pour some *saki* into his own
cup and offer it to her. He can even send her a present—
via an intermediary—and may receive in return a note
of thanks.

Some of the *geisha* ideas of entertainment at such
banquets consist of party games which may well seem
naïve to the foreigner.

The *geisha* has an extremely elaborate wardrobe and

she is supervised by an *okami-san*. *Geishas* are best seen at Kyoto, which is noted for a number of special *geisha* dances originating from *Kabuki*, folk dances and puppet ballads. These take place in Kyoto's theatres, often at the Gion Corner.

Music

The common complaint by foreigners against Japanese music is that it is monotonous; and indeed it takes time for the ear to become accustomed to the subtle changes in harmony and the simplicity of the melody.

Japanese music has borrowed both from China and Korea, and it has developed on a dual level of folk and of court. The *gagaku* music, or literally the authorised, elegant music, began to acquire its present characteristics in the eleventh century. It covers dance rhythms, and harmonies from wind and string instruments. Today it is patronised by the Emperor, who maintains a school of some twenty-five *gagaku* musicians. Other styles grew up out of folk origins or around the *Kabuki* or *Noh* theatres. In the seventeenth and eighteenth centuries a popular form of banquet entertainment developed from three instruments, the *koto*, the *shamisen* and the *shakuhachi*.

The *koto* is like a zither and was introduced from China some 1,200 years ago. No chords are played but instead two tones heard simultaneously make intervals of fifths, fourths, minor thirds and major seconds. The thirteen strings are plucked with the thumb, forefinger and middle finger (shielded by a small piece of ivory). The *koto* usually accompanies singing. The *shamisen* originally came from East Asia via China and has a similar range to the *koto*. Made traditionally from stretched catskin and played with an ivory plectrum, it overtook another string instrument, the *biwa*, in popularity during the seventeenth century. The *shakuhachi* is a type of flute.

Western music has been adopted on a large scale

and there are a number of philharmonic orchestras. The young have, not surprisingly, been strongly attracted to pop music. Concerts in Tokyo usually take place at the Higya Hall, the Ueno Festival Hall and the Sankei Hall.

The Japanese garden

Japanese gardens are different in concept and design from those in the West. City planners have been careful to incorporate gardens and parks into towns, and it is possible to see examples of various types of garden almost anywhere in Japan.

Compared with Western garden designers, the Japanese make no attempt at symmetry. The emphasis is on the natural—a perfect blending with nature which refines and enhances the environment. Traditionally, water in the form of a lake, waterfall, rivulet or stream, has been a central feature; flowers take second place to shrubs and trees. The aim of certain types of garden is to let flowers seed themselves, while attention is paid to trees, shrubs, mosses and lichens. The colour in the garden rarely comes from flowers, mostly from the subtle variations of leaf or blossom and the reflection of water.

Too much can be read into the symbolism and meaning of the various parts of the garden, and many visitors have made them appear more esoteric than their creators probably intended. However, there have always been elements of symbolism. For instance, an island in the middle of a lake represents the holy mountain of happiness. Again there are certain traditions in design; for instance, water flows towards the right.

Most of the traditions and symbolism began to be formulated in the thirteenth and fourteenth centuries, incorporating early ideas of the central lake, fishing pavilions, bridges and courtyards lined with bushes (*senzai*). During this period the garden was transformed from its purely functional purpose, recreation and repose, to something which touched finer sensibilities, and accordingly the design became more aesthetic. The aim was to incorporate nature yet elaborate upon it.

Parallel to this development was the influence of Zen Buddhism which was responsible for the introduction of the dry-landscape style, *Kare-sansui*. This developed from the way the traditional lake was transformed into an area of sand, delicately raked to demonstrate the variations of water. In effect Zen reduced the various elements of nature to refined symbols: bare rocks represented mountains. Without a thorough knowledge of Zen, this type of dry garden might leave the visitor a

The Kenroku Garden Park at Kanazawa.

little cold. But many have found this the most moving of all Japanese gardens. One of the best examples is at the Ryoanji Temple, Kyoto.

Another whole series of garden designs grew up round the Japanese tea ceremony, which later led to the appearance of elaborate pagodas, pavilions and far more extravagant treatment of flowers and shrubs. Nevertheless in the tea garden the tree still predominated, well illustrated in the way the *bonsai* or dwarf trees were cultivated. The finest example of the tea garden is at the Katsura Imperial Villa on the outskirts of Kyoto. It was built in the seventeenth century (Edo period) by Prince Tomohito as an escape from the world of warrior politics. Now it is the property of the Imperial Household and visitors must apply to the Kyoto Office of the Imperial Household Agency for an entry permit.

The tea ceremony

The tea ceremony has lost most of its spiritual quality nowadays and is primarily a social occasion. None the less, it is still practised and offers a good opportunity for a visitor to appreciate the Japanese garden (the ceremony is usually performed in a small arbour in a fine garden) and the simple but refined environment of Japanese living.

The ceremony first became popular among the warrior class in the fifteenth century and incorporated Zen philosophy which required great concentration of mind and dignity of bearing. Traditionally the number of persons present does not exceed five, the tea-set—usually of great antiquity—being brought in while the people assemble in front of the tea pavilion. The tea-set includes the *cha-ire,* a kettle; the *cha-wan,* a communal tea bowl which is passed from hand to hand, each time wiped with a piece of paper; the *cha-sen*, a sort of whisk which is used to stir the tea at the first round before *usa-cha,* or clear tea, is served. The *cha-shaku,* a delicate spoon of bamboo, is also an essential part of the set.

The actual tea drinking is preceded by a light meal. Conversation is at first meant to be limited to formal comment on the surroundings, in particular on the flower arrangements. After the clear tea has been served, conversation can become general. All the time those involved have to remain kneeling in the ceremonial position in front of the table. Seating is strictly according to age or distinction.

The bath

In modern Japanese hotels mixed bathing no longer exists and in those towns where it is still practised it is usually confined to the young or the elderly. Visitors who dislike the idea of communal bathing—or of exposing themselves—can easily acquire rooms with their own private bathrooms.

The bath is usually taken before dining, and the visitor undresses in his bedroom in the presence of a servant who is there to wrap him in a kimono. Once the visitor enters the bath he is meant to remove all clothes, although for the first few moments he can hide his modesty with a small towel which is offered. However, the towel has to make do for washing as well as drying (although 'mopping' would be more correct). Before the main bath is entered the body must be washed in a small tub or *oke*. Baths vary in size but are usually like diminutive swimming pools.

The water is extremely hot by Western standards, averaging around 106 degrees Fahrenheit (40 degrees Centigrade). In theory there should be two swims or 'immersions', interspersed by more washing in the tub (or shaving or washing of hair if desired). However, some may find the water so hot and the atmosphere so steamy that one dip will be enough. In this atmosphere it is difficult to dry properly; indeed the bather is meant to perspire gently. To absorb perspiration a *yukata* or cotton gown is worn.

Judo

Judo, invented in 1878, is a mixture of the various schools of *jujitsu*. Although the aim is to defeat the opponent, the emphasis is on physical exercise and not on the traditional samurai spirit of combat. The sport has its headquarters at the Kodakan sports stadium in Tokyo, although it can be seen in most cities. Over four million Japanese are estimated to practise judo. The main championships take place in the autumn.

Kendo

Kendo is the Japanese equivalent of fencing. Although banned for a time after World War I, the sport has recently regained popularity. It originated in Nara and was known to have been practised in the eighth century. The samurai later adopted it. Under the Tokugawa dictatorship, from the seventeenth to the nineteenth centuries, a form of bamboo sabre was introduced. The body became protected by armour and the face by a mask. The aim of the contest is to strike the opponent on the head, neck, trunk or hand. An unusual feature is the way the fighters shout and grunt, apparently to frighten their adversary. Kendo can be seen occasionally at the Kodakan. Many companies have their own clubs.

Sumo

Sumo, Japanese wrestling, is Japan's most unusual sport. It is treated almost as a religion and its origins are suitably legendary with two gods fighting to possess the province of Shimane. Tournaments were recorded as early as the second century and the sport was professional by about the fifteenth century.

The two wrestlers are enormous, looking like a specially-bred race of giants, and seem even bigger as they fight in a small ring (10 foot radius). The aim is to push the other out of the ring or to make his body touch the ground. Weight plays an important part in the fight and the average champion is around 100 kilogrammes (220 lb). The fights tend to be over suddenly; but first this is preceded by the two wrestlers circling each other, 'building up a will to fight'. They wear a special type of loincloth and have their hair knotted in a sort of chignon. Tournaments take place in Tokyo at certain times of the year and last for fifteen days. They are at New Year, in May and in September. Osaka also has tournaments and small tournaments are to be found in the country.

33

Food

There are several basic differences between Japanese cooking and the Western haute cuisine. The most noticeable is the virtual absence of any sauce, the emphasis being on the individual qualities of the raw materials. Where sauce *is* used it is not intended to cover up unexciting items. Soy sauce (made from roasted corn and steamed soya beans mixed with malt-mould and salt water and then fermented) is considered more as a seasoning than a sauce.

Secondly, there is little attempt to serve out-of-season food. In addition the Japanese prefer to offer small helpings and each item is carefully cut into small pieces; and although oils and fats are kept to a minimum in preparations, liberal use is made of seasoning. The principal seasonings are salt, fermented soya paste *(miso),* thickened soy sauce *(shoya)* and vinegar. Pepper is scarcely used.

Because of the great care in presentation and of what, to Western palates, are unfamiliar ingredients, Japanese food might often prove less appetising than it looks.

The basic stock of Japanese cooking is a clear soup made of *konbu* seaweed, dried bonito fish, and water. Beverages accompanying a meal are limited to *sake*—rice wine mixed with malt, the quality varying considerably depending on the method of fermentation, the water, and the rice-grain—beer and tea. Occasionally a strong coarse alcohol, *shochu*, is produced.

Traditionally, sea-food has predominated, ranging from fish and shellfish to seaweeds. The main ways of eating fish are *sushi* (raw fish with rice), *sashami* (raw fish moistened with soy sauce) and *tempura*, which is a form of deep frying. The materials are dipped in a batter of flour and eggs then immersed in vegetable oil, after which they are placed on paper to soak up excess oil. Before serving they are dipped in a mixture of soup stock and soy sauce.

Although meat is coming within the reach of most Japanese pockets, it is still expensive and good steaks are confined to expensive restaurants. Steaks, however, are extremely tender, due to careful attention—which includes the cattle being fed on beer. *Batayaki* is a traditional way of serving beef where a pot is placed over a small gas flame to allow a light covering of grease to fry slices of meat. The meat is then dipped into a vessel of grated radish and soy sauce. Then vegetables are also fried with the meat, the vegetables usually consisting of mushrooms, egg-plant and onion. There are a large number of dishes cooked on similar lines to the European stewpot principle whereby titbits of meat and vegetables are thrown into a soup stock. Variation is added by giving guests individual cups with soy sauce, vinegar, grated ginger and minced green onion. This is used particularly when sliced chicken and chicken-livers are thus cooked *(mizutaki)*.

The much-famed *sukiyaki* has achieved a popularity outside Japan (probably because it resembles closest Western dishes) which belies its significance within the country. Leeks, spinach, mushrooms, bean-curd, edible chrysanthemums and vermicelli are lightly cooked in a soup stock with soy sauce, *sake* and sugar. The guest then picks out the items of his choice and dips them in his own bowl of raw eggs.

Rice in Japanese-style restaurants is not eaten until all the main-course dishes have been finished. This is because Japanese men do not eat rice while drinking beer or *sake*. Rice is usually accompanied by a choice of pickled vegetables. The last course is normally *misoshiru*—a soy bean paste soup.

Most restaurants are not used to dealing with foreigners. Some of the less expensive restaurants have large displays of the principal dishes they are offering. Most restaurants tend to specialise in particular styles of cooking, whether it be *tempura* or simply the type of ingredients like chicken or raw fish. There are, of course, a number of Western-style restaurants and all

A traditional Japanese meal.

the big hotels have European cuisines or suitably adapted versions of Japanese cooking.

The Japanese eat early. Guests invited for dinner are usually asked to arrive between 17.30 and 18.30, and the whole party is likely to be over by 22.30. This does not mean that the evening has ended; for the visitor is often taken on to a club, music hall or nightclub. Most restaurants close well before midnight and night life tends to stop similarly early, although there are bars which stay open until the small hours.

JAPAN
businessman's
guide

Mount Fuji at dusk.

34

Journey to Japan

In keeping with its status as the third leading country in the world economically, and one of the world's major international trading nations, Japan is very hospitable to visiting businessmen from other countries. The formalities of entering the country are comparatively simple and liberal; the business visitor planning his first trip need fear no problems. In the ordinary way, for a short stay, he will not need even a visa. Citizens of some countries such as Britain, West Germany, Switzerland and Austria, are allowed up to six months of visaless residence. The limit is three months for citizens of several other countries, including Argentina, Belgium, Canada, Finland, France, Greece, Italy, Luxembourg, Netherlands, Norway, Pakistan, Spain, Sweden, Tunisia and Turkey. Businessmen of other countries do not normally have any difficulty in obtaining a visa for any period they wish to visit.

All visitors who intend to stay more than sixty days in the country should, on arrival, register at the Municipal Office in the district where they are staying temporarily, and obtain an Alien Registration Card. In practice, all applications for temporary residence are examined on their merits, on an individual basis, but any visitor on legitimate business should have no difficulty obtaining permission to stay for as long as may be necessary to complete it. The authorities are always prepared to consider applications for an extension of the stay beyond the original period, if this would be advisable for the applicant.

On the other hand, any businessman who has reason to expect that he will want to stay longer in the country than the basic three-to-six month period, would be well advised to acquire a visa at the outset. Such a step is necessary for anyone who intends to work in Japan.

Japanese Embassies

Australia	3, Tennyson Crescent, Forrest, Canberra, A.C.T.
Belgium	31, Avenue des Art, Brussels, 4.
Canada	Fuller Building, 75, Albert Street, Ottawa, 4, Ontario.
Denmark	Biblioteksgaarden, Kultorvet 2, 2nd Floor, Copenhagen, K.
France	24, rue Greuze, Paris, 16.
Germany	Kölner Strasse 139, Bad Godesberg.
Italy	Via Virginio Orsini 18, Rome.
Netherlands	Rustenburgweg No. 2, The Hague.
South Africa	Consulate-General of Japan: 1st Floor, United Dominion Corporation Building, 28, Church Square, Pretoria.
Spain	Paseo de la Habana 7, Madrid, 16.
Sweden	Strandvägen 5B, Stockholm.
Switzerland	42, Helvetiastrasse, Berne.
United Kingdom	46, Grosvenor Street, London, W.1.
United States	2520, Massachusetts Avenue N.W., Washington D.C. 20008.

Such visas are normally issued initially for a three-year period, and are renewable for further periods as they expire. Full details about Japanese visa requirements are available from Japanese Consular offices.

Japanese health regulations stipulate that all foreign visitors must hold a valid International Certificate of Vaccination, showing that they have been inoculated against smallpox within the period of the previous three years. In addition, any visitor who has passed through an area infected with typhoid or cholera will also have to produce a certificate of inoculation against these diseases, as a condition of being admitted.

Currency controls

Japanese currency control regulations also are comparatively liberal. For example a visitor can take into the country any amount of foreign currency, in notes, travellers' cheques, letters of credit, and so on. However, a visitor may not take out of Japan more than 20,000 yen (about 56 dollars or £23). Because of these regulations, it is advisable to declare all holdings of foreign currency on entering the country, whether in the form of notes or travellers' cheques. A record of this amount is then affixed to the passport.

Another document of interest to the foreign visitor, whether or not on business, is the *record of purchase of commodities tax exempt for export*. This is so that certain stores which are designated to sell cameras, transistor radios, jewellery and other goods popular with visitors from abroad free of the purchase tax normally levied on them, may record details of any such purchases on the form. This record is acceptable for verification by Japanese customs authorities at the point of departure.

Hotels and restaurants in the upper price categories in the ordinary way will cash travellers' cheques in foreign currency denominations. Otherwise, the visitor should use the services of the banks.

Bank of Tokyo (main foreign exchange bank)	6, 1-chome, Nihonbashi Hongokucho, Chuo-ku, Tokyo.
Bank of Kobe	56 Naniwa-cho, Ikuta-ku, Kobe.
Daiichi Bank	1, 1-chome, Marunouchi, Chiyoda-ku, Tokyo.
Daiwa Bank	21, 2-chome, Bingo-machi, Higashi-ku, Osaka.
Fuji Bank	6, 1-chome, Ote-machi, Chiyoda-ku, Tokyo.
Industrial Bank of Japan	1-1, 5-chome, Yaesu, Chuo-ku, Tokyo.
Mitsubishi Bank	5, 2-chome, Marunouchi, Chiyoda-ku, Tokyo.
Mitsui Bank	12 Yurakucho, 1-chome, Chiyoda-ku, Tokyo.
Nippon Kangyo Bank	1, 1-chome, Uchisaiwai-cho, Chiyoda-ku, Tokyo.
Sanwa Bank	10, 4-chome, Fushimi-cho, Higashi-ku, Osaka.
Sumitomo Bank	22, 5-chome, Kitahama, Higashi-ku, Osaka.
Tokai Bank	21-24 Nishiki 3-chome, Naka-ku, Nagoya.

Source: Japan Air Lines

Leading American and Western European banks also maintain branches in the Japanese capital and other principal cities.

Normally, the visitor is expected to settle his bills in yen. However, United States, Canadian and Australian dollars, and most Western European currencies, are freely negotiable. Hong Kong dollars which generally are not accepted elsewhere, will be taken by British banks.

Any surplus yen the visitor has on him, up to the legal limit, at the time he leaves the country, normally can be converted into the currency with which he entered; but only once, and only up to the amount recorded by the bank or money changer who makes the conversion.

The climate

The visitor from northern Europe or North America who is in Japan in the period from mid-October to April can expect to be comfortable in the same clothes as he wears at home. Those whose bases are further south will feel the cold, and should take heavier-weight suits and an overcoat for the visit.

In the Japanese spring and autumn, the northerly visitor will need to be more lightly clad than usual; all visitors in the summer season should be equipped with tropical weight clothing. Climate varies also with the location.

Japanese weather

January–March	Cold and dry for long periods
April–May	Fine and dry for long periods
June	Rain, warm
July–August	Humid, hot, overcast
September	Unsettled
October–November	Warm, dry for long periods
December	Cool and dry for long periods

Source: Board of Trade, London

A businessman who expects to attend diplomatic or other formal functions while on his visit to Japan should take formal evening dress in addition to business suits. Japan has excellent laundering and dry cleaning services, which are fast, even if rather expensive; many leading hotels offer same-day service.

European and North American brands of shaving soaps, lotions and toothpastes may cost as much as twice the amount in the country of origin, but there are excellent local equivalents. An electric razor in Japan may need a transformer, as the current in most hotels is 100 volts ac.

Medical services

Medical services are available in all the major cities. Larger hotels can recommend English-speaking doctors and, if needed, dentists.

Hospitals, clinics and chemists

TOKYO

Tokyo Sanatorium Hospital (Seventh Day Adventist)	17-3, 3-chome, Amanuma, Suginami-ku, Tokyo. Tel: 392–6151.
Harajuku Medical Clinic (affiliated with Tokyo Sanatorium Hospital)	11-5 Jingumae, 1-chome, Shibuya-ku, Tokyo. Tel: 401–1282.
Tokyo Medical and Surgical Clinic	Masonic Bldg., 13 Sakae-cho, Shiba, Minato-ku, Tokyo. Tel: 431–4121/9 Ext. 109.
American Pharmacy	Nikkatsu Int'l. Bldg., 1, 1-chome, Yuraku-cho, Chiyoda-ku, Tokyo. Tel: 271–4034/5.
Hill Pharmacy	23 Azabu, Imai-cho, Minato-ku, Tokyo. Tel: 583–5044.

Bluff Hospital	82 Yamate-cho, Naka-ku, Yokohama. Tel: Yokohama 641–6951.
Hill Pharmacy	128, 3-chome, Motomachi, Nakaku, Yokohama. Tel: Yokohama 64–0885/6.

KOBE/OSAKA

Kaisei Hospital	47, 3-chome, Shinohara, Nada-Ku, Kobe. Tel: Kobe 87–5201.
American Pharmacy	3-36 Shimoyamate Dori, Ikuta-ku, Kobe. Tel: Kobe 33–1352, 39–1384.
Yodogawa Christian Hospital	57 Awajimachi, Higashi-Yodogawa-ku, Osaka. Tel: 322–2250.

Source: Japan Air Lines

JETRO

The businessman can gain valuable help in planning his trip to Japan from the Japanese External Trade Organisation (JETRO), which has offices in the major foreign capitals. A government-supported agency that works closely with the Ministry of International Trade and Industry, JETRO's main function is to act as a clearing house of information on goods available for export from Japan, including sponsorship of trade fairs.

JETRO also can give foreign businessmen the names of Japanese firms in their particular fields which might be interested in importing.

Amsterdam	Herengracht 462, Amsterdam C.
Athens	Academia 17.
Belgrade	No. 5, Lackoviceve, Dedinje.
Brussels	479, Avenue Louise, Brussels 5.
Copenhagen	25 Landmaerket, Copenhagen K.
Dusseldorf	Berliner Allee 32.
Hamburg	Colonnaden 72.
London	535 Oxford Street, W.1.
Madrid	Doctor Fleming, 32-8A-92.93, Madrid 16.
Milan	Via G. Puccini 3, 20121.
New York	393 Fifth Avenue.
Oslo	c/o Mr. Knut K. Olsen, Skippergate 27
Paris	c/o Martini Building, 50 Avenue des Champs Elysees.
Stockholm	Valhallavagen 73.
Toronto	151 Bloor Street West
Venice	c/o Palazzo Nuovo di I.N.P.S., Dorsoduro, Rio Nuovo 3500.
Zürich	Stockerstrasse 6, 8002.

35

Getting around

Most businessmen arrive in Japan at Tokyo International Airport, which is about twenty-five miles from the centre of the Japanese capital. The trip to the downtown area, by bus or taxi, takes a little over thirty minutes.

Tokyo is full of excellent hotels. Rates are comparable to European hotels of the same grade.

The foreign visitor is strongly advised to make his reservation in advance, and as much as three or four months ahead of the time he expects to arrive, if possible, in order to be certain of getting the accommodation he wants, in the hotel of his choice. All reservations should indicate the length of the intended stay.

If the itinerary is to include other major Japanese cities advance reservation is particularly important, since top class accommodation tends to be more limited. However, these cities also have their share of excellent Western-style hotels. In the smaller cities, there is usually at least one good hotel run on Western lines. In the event of being unable to find such accommodation, the foreign visitor may enjoy the experience of staying at Japanese *ryokan* (inns). These are famed for their atmosphere and service, and provide a glimpse of the Japanese scene not ordinarily experienced. On arrival guests remove their shoes and city clothes, and

Akasaka Prince	1, Kioicho, Chiyoda-ku.
Azabu Prince	5-40, 3-chome, Minami-Azabu, Minato-ku
Daiei	15, 1-chome, Koishikawa, Bunkyo-ku.
Dai-ichi	2-6, 1-chome, Shimbashi, Minato-ku.
Diamond	25, Ichibancho, Chiyoda-ku.
Fairmont	1-17, 2-chome, Kudan-Minami, Chiyoda-ku.
Ginza Nikko	4-21, 8-chome, Ginza-Nidshi, Chuo-ku.
Ginza Tokyu	5, 5-chome, Ginza-Higashi, Chuo-ku.
Hill Top	1, 1-chome, Kanda Surugadai, Chiyoda-ku.
Imperial	1, 1-chome, Uchisaiwai-cho, Chiyoda-ku.
Kokusai Kanko	1, 1-chome, Marunouchi, Chiyoda-ku.
Marunouchi	1, 1-chome, Marunouchi, Chiyoda-ku.
New Japan	13-8, 2-chome, Nagatacho, Chiyoda-ku.
New Otani	4, Kioicho, Chiyoda-ku.
New Plaza	35-14, 2-chome, Akebonocho, Tachikawa.
Nikkatsu	1, 1-chome, Yurakucho, Chiyoda-ku.
Okura	3, Aoicho, Akasaka, Minato-ku.
Palace	10, 1-chome, Marunouchi, Chiyoda-ku.
San Bancho	1, Sambancho, Chiyoda-ku.
Shiba Park	3, 6-gochi, Shiba Park, Minato-ku.
Takanawa	1-17, 2-chome, Takanawa, Minato-ku.

Takanawa Prince	16-5, 2-chome, Higashi-ve, Taito-ku.
Takara	2-16, Higashieuno, Taito-ku.
Tokyo Grand	1, 2-chome, Nagatacho, Chiyoda-ku.
Tokyo Hilton	10-3, 2-chome, Nagatacho, Chiyoda-ku.
Tokyo Kanko	10-8, 4-chome, Takanawa Minamicho, Minato-ku.
Tokyo Prince	No. 3, Shiba Park, Minato-ku.
Tokyo Station	1, 2-chome, Marunouchi, Chiyoda-ku.
Toshi Center	6, 2-chome, Hirakawacho, Chiyoda-ku.

Source: Board of Trade, London

put on *Yukata*, or cotton gowns, supplied by the house. They also have the opportunity to be initiated into the ritual of the Japanese bath, and sleep on luxurious quilted mattresses laid out on floor mats, although the pillow is often filled with straw.

In every major Japanese city are several restaurants serving Western-style dishes. At these it is possible to lunch or dine alone for as little as 2.4 dollars (£1), but for a business lunch the cost is likely to run as high as 5,000 yen (14 dollars or £5 15s) a head, without wine. European wines are very expensive in Japan, and the much cheaper local wines can be very palatable. A small whisky costs about 1.2 dollars (10s), and a litre bottle of beer about 72 cents (almost 6s). Japanese lager beer is particularly good.

The larger Japanese hotels have rooms at the disposal of foreign businessmen for private lunches, cocktail parties and similar functions. The cost of giving a cocktail party for fifty people in a private room at a prestigious hotel is likely to be around 600 dollars (£250).

One pleasant surprise for the visitor to Japan is

that tipping is much less of a burden than in most countries. Both hotels and restaurants normally add a 10 per cent service charge to the bill, and hotels also add another 10 per cent in tax. Additional gratuities are not generally expected, and may not even be accepted. It is not necessary to tip taxi drivers and barmen, for example.

Tipping guide

Hotels and restaurants	Waiters do not expect any further tipping when service charges and/or taxes are added to the bill. Porters in hotels patronised by foreigners will accept tips but do not necessarily expect them.
Taxi drivers	No tipping.
Barbers/hairdressers	A tip is expected by barbers in hotels but not elsewhere.
Porters, railway and airport	50-100 yen per piece of luggage according to size. In the event of doubt, porters usually say how much they expect.

Source: Board of Trade, London

Communications

Japan has a first-class internal communications network. The businessman who needs to cover as much ground as possible in a limited time, including visits to other cities as well as Tokyo, will probably travel by air. The three main Japanese domestic airlines are Japan Air Lines, which offers a service over the route Tokyo, Sapporo, Osaka to Fukuoka; All Nippon Airways, which connects the capital with Sendai, Sapporo, Nagoya, Kita–Kuyushu, Osaka; and Japan Domestic Airlines, which flies over the route Tokyo, Sapporo,

Fukuoka. All offer frequent, regular daily services, and several smaller airlines provide regular 'feeder' connections. A 5 per cent airport tax is levied on all domestic flights.

A typical Japanese inn: guests have left their shoes on the stone threshold.

The visitor with a little more time to spare may opt to go by train, especially sampling one of the crack flyers, such as the *Hikari,* which covers the 556 kilometres between Tokyo and Osaka in three hours ten minutes, stopping also at Nagoya and Kyoto. Only slightly less swift is the *Kodama* which covers the same distance in four hours, but with more intermediate stops. The former service provides twenty-five and the latter twenty-six trains daily in each direction. All the trains are air-conditioned, with restaurant and buffet services, and with facilities for two-way telephone communication en route with Tokyo, Nagoya and Osaka. It is possible to reserve seats in advance, and this is absolutely necessary at rush hours, weekends, and other peak seasons.

Long distance road travel by foreigners with limited time is not recommended, as outside the big cities the highways tend to be congested and are not always well surfaced—though an extensive network of new, modern motorways is presently under construction.

The major cities have excellent public transportation systems, including cheap bus and streetcar services. The only problem for the foreigner is that their signs are in Japanese only. On the other hand, signs on the underground railway services in Tokyo, Osaka and Nagoya also are posted in English. The fare is about 8 cents (8*d*) per stage, and, as in other big cities internationally, the subway is the quickest of all ways to get around.

However, probably the foreign businessman will do most of his big city travelling in a taxi. In this connection, it is important for him to have his directions written in Japanese, including, if possible, telephone numbers. Most Japanese taxi drivers do not speak English, and so require as precise as possible directions in their own tongue. It is reasonably easy to pick up a cruising taxi by day though it is often hard at night. If in difficulty one can call a taxi by phone. For this reason, the best policy for the visitor is to seek the help

Ginza Line	Shibuya to Asakusa via Akasaka, Ginza and Ueno.
Marunouchi Line	Ogikubo to Ikebukuro via Shinjuku, Ginza Tokyo Station.
Route No. 1 Line	Oshiage to Daimon via Asakusabashi and Shimbashi.
Hibiya Line (Route No. 2)	Kitasenju to Hiyoshi via Ueno and Nakameguro.
Tozai Line (Route No. 5)	Mitaka to Otemachi.

Source: Japan Air Lines

of his hotel, a restaurant, or the business contact he is about to leave, in hiring a taxi and indicating his next destination.

Taxis in Japan come in three sizes. The largest American-style vehicles are intended mainly for the foreign visitors, and it is possible to economise by hiring one of the medium-sized or smaller cars. For two kilometres the charge is about 36 cents (3s) for a large car, 30 cents (2s 6d) for a medium, and 24 cents (2s) for a small car. After that the rate is about 6 cents (6d) for every additional 330 metres.

Somewhat similar advice applies to the use of the telephone. Get help whenever possible. In hotels, English-speaking operators can help with placing calls. In Tokyo an English-speaking operator is on call to help with locating directory numbers; however, she cannot be called from a telephone box. English-speaking operators for overseas calls can be reached by dialling 109. For local calls from pay telephones the charge is a 10 yen coin.

International cables may be sent from the offices of Kokusai Denshin Denwa Co. Ltd, and of Nippon

Denshin Denwa Hosha, domestic communications services, and also from larger post offices in the principal cities. Over a dozen private telegraph circuits on an all-cable route between London and Tokyo have been provided for certain banks, trading companies and similar organisations, and similar arrangements exist for other countries. Express telegraph rates are double the ordinary rates.

Telex booths are available at the main offices and branches of the Kokusai Denshin Denwa Co. Ltd, in Tokyo, Osaka, Yokohama and Nagoya. In all, domestic and international telex facilities are available covering 159 cities in Japan and eighty countries in Asia, Europe, North and South America.

Foreign businessmen can arrange to have their telephone, telegraph and other communications expenses charged to their firms at home, or make use of the facilities afforded by international credit cards.

Sightseeing

Japan has its fair share of sights for the tourist and off-duty businessman to see. Here are some of them:

TOKYO
Japan's capital is home of more than 12 million people and the world's largest city. It is the centre of government, commerce, sports, education and the lively arts, both ancient and modern.

The Imperial Palace   Residence of the Emperor since 1868. Open to the public only on 2 January and on 29 April, the Emperor's birthday. Its famed 'Nijubashi' bridge, however, may be visited any day, and its moat and gardens are the major landmark of central Tokyo.

The National Diet   Seat of Japan's parliament. It is surrounded by broad parks—a 'green zone' created to enhance the national capital.

Meiji Shrine   Dedicated to the father of modern Japan, the Emperor Meiji. Wooded precincts surround the shrine proper, mecca for many annual festivals. Next door, in the Outer Gardens, are enormous sporting facilities—venue of the 1964 Olympics.

Tokyo Tower   Erected as the world's tallest tower in 1958, it resembles the Eiffel Tower but uses far less steel. Standing 333 metres (1,083 feet) high, it is built to withstand earthquakes and typhoons. Its observation platform offers an excellent view of Tokyo.

The Ginza   Fashionable shopping and entertainment area, with department stores, neon signs and 'go-go' bars and clubs.

Ueno Park   Japan's largest park. In its grounds of

Lake Ashi in the Hakone National Park.

210 acres is everything for the tourist: the Tokyo National Museum, the National Science Museum, Ueno Library, Japan's largest zoo, the Tokyo Metropolitan Theatre and the seventeenth-century Toshogu Shrine. In spring its cherry trees in blossom are a great attraction.

Asakusa   Tokyo's traditional amusement centre. Asakusa Kannon Temple, the Kokusai Theatre and Nakamise shopping arcade highlight its attractions.

Kabukiza   The theatre at which to watch the Kabuki performances (see p. 192).

YOKOHAMA

Next door to Tokyo, this major port city was opened to foreign trade in 1859.

The Heian Shrine at Kyoto.

Marine Tower A 340-foot observation tower over-looking Yamashita Park and the harbour.

Silk Centre Modern hotel with a museum of precious silk—still traded there daily in its auction hall.

The Bluff Traditional home of foreign residents since Japan reopened its doors to the outside world in 1868.

Isogo Its new dockyards build the world's largest ships—tankers from 100,000 tons upwards.

KAMAKURA

A seaside town forty miles from Tokyo that was once a Shogun's headquarters in the Middle Ages. A popular resort in summer.

Great Buddha The Daibutsu or Great Buddha stands out of doors in a classic park. The Buddha was cast of bronze in 1252 and is 42 feet high.

Tsurugaoka Hachiman Shrine One of Japan's most famous Shinto shrines, site of several annual festivals.

FUJI-HAKONE-IZU NATIONAL PARK

Playground for residents of Tokyo and the surrounding suburbs. In this 366-square-mile park are volcanoes, hot springs, placid lakes, excellent inns and, now, golf courses.

Mt Fuji Soaring 12,397 feet, it is best seen in winter, when gusty winds clear clouds from its peak. During July and August thousands of pilgrims are attracted to its sacred summit.

Hakone and Fuji Five Lakes At the approach to Mt Fuji, this area is of great historical and scenic interest. Miyanoshita, site of the Fujiya Hotel, is the centre of sightseeing activity. Cable cars ply across gorges to add to this area's spectacle.

Izu Peninsula Its steep slopes are terraced for tangerine trees and tea bushes.

Atami In a cove at the neck of Izu Peninsula, this hot-spring resort is Japan's mecca for honeymooners. The spa is reached by the new Bullet Express Tokaido from Tokyo and is a gateway to the whole Fuji-Hakone area.

NIKKO

A two-hour train trip from Tokyo, Nikko is one of Japan's most spectacular sights. Giant trees, waterfalls, lakes, and meadows provide the setting for shrines, bridges, gates and temples. These were built in honour

Himeji Castle.

of Ieyasu, founder of the Tokugawa Shogunate that ruled Japan from 1603 to 1867. The 'Sleeping Cat', and the Three Monkeys, depicting 'Hear no evil, speak no evil, see no evil', are popular attractions. Lake Chuzenji, above the major shrines, offers boating, fishing and swimming in summer; skating in winter.

Toshogu Shrine Most lavish shrine in Japan. Its architecture reflects the uninhibited spirit of the 9,000 craftsmen who gilded it with six acres of gold leaf three centuries ago.

Sacred Bridge At the entrance to Toshogu shrine, this bridge is crossed only twice a year—by Imperial messengers during the spring and autumn Grand Festivals.

Yomeimon Gate A national treasure with intricate carving and lacquer and gold embellishments. Only the warrior class could pass through it in feudal times.

Kegon Fall The second-highest waterfall in Japan. Its waters come from Lake Chuzenji, and a splendid view of them can be seen from an observation platform at the waterfall's base.

Nasu A popular hot-spring resort situated in the northernmost extreme of the Nikko National Park.

NAGOYA

A major industrial city on the Tokaido road between Tokyo and Kyoto, and the centre of the motor industry, this is a centre for pottery, cloisonné and other handi-crafts. The port is also the gateway to the Grand Ise Shrines.

Nagoya Castle Built in the seventeenth century by Ieyasu Tokugawa, the citadel is Nagoya's major landmark.

Grand Ise Shrines The most sacred of all Imperial Shrines, dedicated to the Sun Goddess, divine ancestress of the Imperial line.

Pearl Island Reached by hydrofoil from Nagoya, this

island is where Mikimoto first succeeded in producin
cultured pearls in 1893.

KYOTO

Ancient cultural capital of Japan, Kyoto first held the
seat of government in AD 794. Today some 600 shrines
and 1,600 temples reflect its past. Handicrafts are the
most elegant in Japan and its festival season lasts
all year-round.

Gold Pavilion   Three-storeyed gilded temple of the
Zen sect.

Heian Shrine   Brilliant vermilion pillared shrine built
in 1895 to commemorate Kyoto's 1,100th anniversary.

Nijo Castle   The Grand Hall of this 350-year-old
fortress is decorated lavishly in gold and damascene.

Old Imperial Palace   Dignified simplicity marks the
architecture of this site of Imperial coronations.

Sanjusangendo Temple   Built in the thirteenth century,
this is the temple of 'a thousand and one Buddhas'.

Higashi Honganji Temple   One of the largest Buddhist
temples in Japan, it is one of the headquarters of the
Jodo-Shinshu sect, whose membership totals nearly
20 million.

Kiyomizu Temple   Founded in the eighth century on a
mountainside overlooking Kyoto. The present structure,
dating from the seventeenth century, juts out spectacu-
larly on a cliff. Pilgrims are attracted to its ice-cold
holy waters.

Ryoanji Temple   Famous for its gardens, including the
Zen Buddhist one with rocks in a sea of raked gravel.

Gion   The downtown area in which Kyoto's famous
Geisha entertainers live and work. Some of the city's
finest restaurants are cloistered here.

NARA

Next door to Kyoto, this was Japan's first permanent
capital, established in AD 710.

NARA PARK   Hundreds of tame deer roam the 1,250-
acre grounds of this preserve.

226

Kasuga Shrine A bright vermilion shrine whose corridors are hung with bronze lanterns donated by believers.

The Bunraku Puppet Theatre at Osaka.

Kofukuji Temple Traditional tutelary temple of the Fujiwara shoguns.

Tokaiji Temple The world's largest wooden structure houses the 72-foot-tall Great Buddha, biggest in Japan.

Nara Suburbs Horyuji Temple is the main treasure in this area. It is the world's oldest wooden building, constructed in AD 607. Many relics are contained in the Main Hall.

Yakushiji Temple Built by the Emperor Temmu late in the seventh century, the temple is dedicated to the Yakushi Buddha of Medicine.

OSAKA

Japan's second-largest city is the important commercial and industrial capital of Western Japan and the terminus of the Tokaido Line. Its most famous historical figure is Hideyoshi Toyotomi, who built his castle here in the sixteenth century. Because he appreciated the value of commerce and industry, prosperity has flourished since ancient times. Today, in fact, the Osaka merchant is known throughout Japan for his keen business sense. Now nearly 3·5 million people live in the Osaka area.

Osaka Castle The largest castle in Japan, built in the seventeenth century by Hideyoshi Toyotomi.

Bunraku Theatre Home of the puppet stage art in which black-robed manipulators operate dolls of nearly human size.

Shinsaibashi The world's largest covered pedestrian shopping arcade, with restaurants, bars and *pachinco* saloons. The centre of Osaka night life, brilliantly lit with neon signs.

Tsutenkaku A 340-foot tower that offers a magnificent view of the city and Inland Sea.

Industrial Tours A selection of informative tours of leading Osaka industrial facilities are offered to individuals and groups of commercial visitors.

KOBE

The Orient's largest port faces the emerald waters of the

Inland Sea twenty miles from Osaka. At its back are the steep slopes of Mt Rokko. Motomachi Street is the main shopping area.

Himeji Castle   Some thirty-five miles west of Kobe, the fourteenth century Heron Castle is one of Japan's most beautiful, with gleaming white walls.

36

Social conventions

If the formalities involved in visiting Japan pose few problems for the businessman, the country observes a code of business and social conventions which is exceptional, and not likely to be duplicated in most other countries with which he will become involved. Advance knowledge of these conventions is an important function of any planning, since the businessman from abroad will be expected to conform. A mission admirably conceived in all other respects, could founder from a failure fully to observe Japanese etiquette.

Personal contacts, important in any international business dealings, are absolutely vital in Japan. Before leaving his own country, the businessman from abroad should spend some time and trouble ensuring that he will have the right kind of contacts on arrival. Having established them, he will find doors opening to him at every turn. Lacking them, he may beat against them in vain. He should not decline any introductions offered, even if they appear to have little connection with the purpose of his visit.

The Japanese business world tends to be a comparatively close-knit society, both among business firms themselves, and in its close relationships with banks, government departments, the civil service, and other official agencies. This is a great advantage if one can obtain the right entrée, and a handicap in the event of failure. Thus, any introduction into the elite power structure of the country, is valuable. If the contact himself is not directly connected with the visitor's business, undoubtedly he will have friends who are. Thus establishing the right contacts can be the most important of all preliminary exercises.

Indirect approach

A businessman going to Japan should allow more time than for visits to most countries with which he does business. This is because the Japanese prefer the oblique to the direct approach in such transactions, which are surrounded with certain formalities and courtesies rarely used elsewhere. On this subject, the British Embassy in Tokyo advises: 'It is wise, therefore, to give at least twice as long for an initial visit to Japan as would be given to any other industrialised country. In particular, do not expect concrete results from a visit of less than a week.'

An almost obligatory convention in Japan is the exchange of business cards on introduction. For this reason, the foreign visitor should be well supplied with such credentials, if possible with the name of his firm and other key data inscribed in Japanese. Japan Air Lines offers a Name-card Service, through which a foreign businessman can obtain bi-lingual calling cards, with the data in the visitor's language on one side, and in Japanese on the other. These can be ordered simply by filling out a form at any JAL office. The printed cards can then be awaiting the visitor on his arrival at the airline's International Passenger Centre at Kasumi-gaseki, in Tokyo. JAL advises that orders be placed at least two weeks in advance. As a rough guide, the airline recommends a supply of 300 cards for a two-week visit, assuming also their use to establish identity at hotels, restaurants, stores. Additional supplies of cards, if needed, can always be quickly and cheaply supplied by local printers.

The foreign businessman may be in some doubt as to how to greet his Japanese associates on introduction. The Japanese are widely portrayed as a people much given to courtesy bowing. However, these days, a Western-style handshake is equally acceptable. The foreign visitor should respond to whatever approach is initiated by the other party. It is important that visiting businessmen follow up any introductions afforded them, and punctiliously keep any appointments made. If encouraged by the reception, the visitor should not hesitate to reciprocate, as this will be expected.

Much business is done in Japan over lunch or dinner, and such functions often can have much more significance in Japan than elsewhere. The British Embassy in Tokyo advises that, provided the right personal relationships have been established with the right contact: 'A gentleman's agreement with a senior Japanese, given over the dinner table, can be as good as, if not better than a detailed legal agreement drawn up after hours of quibbling over every word.' The Embassy also adds the cautionary reminder that: 'A Japanese who concludes such a gentleman's agreement expects that the spirit will be honoured on both sides. Thus, he will expect deliveries to be made on the dates promised, at agreed price and of quality specified. He will not understand if trouble with labour, subcontractors, and the like, causes delays, because this generally does not happen in Japan.'

Hours of Business

Banks	09.00 hours to 15.00 hours Monday to Friday; 09.00 hours to noon Saturday.
Commercial offices	usually 09.00 hours to 17.30 hours Monday to Friday. A large number of offices are open on Saturday mornings.

Department stores	10.00 hours to 18.00 hours (The weekly holiday is usually on Monday, occasionally Thursday; retail establishments usually close on Sunday, Monday or Thursday).
Government Departments	10.00 hours to 16.00 hours.

Source: Board of Trade, London

Public holidays

1 January	New Year's Day.
2, 3, 4 January	Bank Holidays (all commercial firms are closed).
15 January	Adults' Day.
11 February	National Foundation Day.
21 March	Vernal Equinox Day (date changes from year to year).
29 April	The Emperor's Birthday.
1 May	May Day (most manufacturers closed, service firms open).
3 May	Constitution Memorial Day.
5 May	Children's Day.

(*Note* From 29 April–5 May is 'Golden Week'. Some firms remain closed the entire time. Some manufacturers close for a week during the summer.)

15 September	Respect of the Aged Day.
24 September	Autumnal Equinox Day (date changes from year to year).
10 October	Physical Culture Day.
3 November	Culture Day.
23 November	Labour Thanksgiving Day.
28 December	New Year's Holiday begins (lasts about 5 to 10 days).

Source: Japan Air Lines

Parties

In addition to formal functions such as business lunches and dinners, the businessman from abroad is likely to be invited to informal gatherings in Japan. The Japanese are great party givers, and the visitor should not fail to accept an invitation to a party, as this can be very helpful in cementing business relationships.

A special feature of the Japanese scene are all-male parties often presided over by professional *geisha*. Such gatherings can be very lively, and festivity of this kind is not frowned upon in Japan. However, the *geisha* emphatically are not included in the high jinks. They are professional entertainers and conversationalists, highly trained in such arts as singing, dancing, folding paper games, and so on. Their gracious offices of serving food, lighting cigarettes, and the like, implies no more than courtesy, and the foreigner should follow the lead of his hosts in treating them with decorum.

A special favour, and a sign that things are going well, is an invitation from a Japanese business associate to visit his home. The most important rule to remember for such social occasions is that shoes should be removed on entering the house; this also is a convention which many Japanese-style restaurants observe. A change to house slippers generally is permissible. However in buildings of wholly Japanese style, even slippers normally are worn only in the passages, and the visitor should expect to enter rooms only in his socks.

Most Japanese meals consist of several small dishes, including many often unfamiliar to the Western visitor, notably the local delicacy of raw fish. The naturally polite Japanese host will no doubt understand if the foreign guest declines such specialities. On the other hand, he will be gratified if an attempt is made to sample them. Actually, many foreigners find raw fish appetising, even delicious.

At parties or family gatherings, it is advisable for the businessman guest to wait for the host to raise the question of business, if he chooses to do so at that time. If the opportunity thus presents itself, it is quite in order to enter into such a discussion. But failure to do so should not be deplored. The occasion itself will have enhanced the relationship.

A Japanese meal usually ends with the eating of fruit, and an end to drinking is normally marked by the serving of rice. A Japanese host is likely to signify that it is time for a guest to leave by announcing that the latter's car is waiting. Such hints should not be ignored. A letter of thanks for any hospitality should be sent, and will be greatly appreciated by the host.

The foreign businessman who has been entertained by a Japanese associate is not obliged to reciprocate immediately, or even during the course of his visit. His turn will come when the Japanese is a guest in his own country. However, if the visitor wishes to return the hospitality forthwith, he probably would be wise to do so at a Western-style restaurant, of which there are any number of excellent ones in the major cities of the country. Japanese-style restaurants can be very expensive, one needs an introduction to them, and it takes experience to become familiar with the menu. Japanese businessmen are, in any case, used to being entertained Western-style. The cost of such entertainment can, again, be quite high, and even create a problem for visitors on a limited budget, which is another reason for the visitor to postpone the return courtesy until he can offer it in his own community at home.

Exchanging gifts

What he can do meanwhile is to participate appropriately in the Japanese custom of exchanging gifts. This convention has a whole lore of its own, even extending to the manner of presenting and even wrapping gifts, which the foreigner cannot hope to master.

The basic rule is never to refuse such gifts from business associates, which should not be regarded as bribes or an attempt to win favours, but as tokens of esteem to cement the relationship. The foreign visitor who brings such tokens of his own will create a favourable impression; otherwise, he should by all means reciprocate for any gifts received on his next visit, or send them in the interval. Such gifts need not be expensive, and may, indeed, consist of pens, pencils, paperweights, calendars, and the like, including advertising material regularly dispensed for promotional purposes. It is the gift itself, not the value of it, that is important. However, a valuable present should be returned in kind.

In modern times, the Japanese have become among the world's leading exponents of doing business on the golf course. They are enthusiastic about the game, and many play it well. But in the business milieu the standard of competition is not all that important, and any foreign businessman familiar with the game should not hesitate to accept an invitation to a round. He can take his golf clubs with him to Japan, secure they have a part to play in his business affairs. If he does not have them, his host will lend clubs, or they can be hired. It may be putting things too strongly to say that the businessman who is a non-golfer loses face. But a mutual enthusiasm for the sport, and a mutually enjoyable session on the course, can help importantly to clinch business transactions launched in formal sessions. Japan has many excellent golf courses, on which girl caddies are a unique feature.

At the same time, the Japanese are a highly cultured people, and businessmen are usually knowledgeable about and devoted to the arts, such as the theatre, dance, painting. The foreigner who takes the trouble to inform himself on important aspects of the country's culture will certainly win goodwill. Even if not so informed he will enhance his status by taking an intelligent interest in such outstanding cultural institutions as the theatrical art of *Kabuki*, in which the female parts also are performed by male actors; and the

next decision will be whether to use a domestic or a foreign agency. Strong arguments can be offered in favour of either. Japanese trading firms claim that only they thoroughly understand all the problems of the highly complex Japanese market, and that they are at an advantage through their contacts with local banks, government officials, and others of influence in decision making. They also have close links with all parts of the country, and can often offer favourable credit terms. In addition, the Japanese trading companies tend to be much larger than the foreign competition, and to have more offices and branches. Their power can be assessed from the fact that the top dozen or so of them control about 50 per cent of all the nation's imports and exports.

Against them it can be argued that they tend to be organised into well-defined product groups, and that any one trading company is not greatly interested in items outside its own group, with which it does business almost exclusively. Not all, however, are so group-oriented.

The arguments in favour of turning to a foreign-owned trading company are that it can take the viewpoint of the exporting firm as well as that of the Japanese importer, and is more likely to be familiar with the former's problems. It can be more impartial in handling negotiations with Japanese clients. The leading foreign trading companies are also buyers from as well as sellers to Japan, and so have an excellent market insight. They employ high-calibre Japanese, well connected in the business community, knowing their way around the 'old boy' circuit, in positions of responsibility.

The individual businessman should investigate the situation for himself, and decide which type of agency would best suit his product in all circumstances.

Payment

Japanese agents normally arrange to pay for imports

either by means of an irrevocable letter of credit or ordinary usance terms, up to 120 days, on either a documents-against-payment or a documents-against-acceptance basis. If capital equipment is involved, however, the importer will have to obtain an import permit from the Japanese Ministry of Finance, and he may, therefore, ask for extended terms beyond usance facilities.

Japan has no established channel of debt collection, though arbitration facilities do exist. In the event of debt collection problems, it may be necessary to seek legal advice, which can be expensive.

Businessmen saying goodbye: formal courtesies have a place even in the busy world of commerce.

Some Tokyo legal advisers

*Adachi	409–415 Sumitomo Building, 1–2 Marunouchi, Chiyoda-ku, Tokyo. Tel: 281–5389/6173.
Anderson, Mori and Rabinowitz	Zenkyoren Building, 7,2-chome, Hirakawa-cho, Chiyoda-ku, Tokyo. Tel: 265–3291.
Thomas L. Blackmore	Room 912, Iino Building, 1–1,2-chome, Uchisaiwai-cho, Chiyoda, Tokyo. Tel: 503–5571.
Furness, Capron, Sato and Matsui	311 Fukoku Building, 2–2,2-chome, Uchisaiwai-cho, Chiyoda-ku, Tokyo. Tel: 591–4124/7.
*Braun, Moriya and Hoaski	Room 911, Iino Building, 1–1,2-chome, Uchisaiwai-cho, Chiyoda-ku, Tokyo. Tel: 504–0251.
*Hill, Betts, Yamaoka, Freehill and Longscope	8th Floor, Yamaguchi Building, 1–1,2-chome, Shinbashi, Minato-ku, Tokyo. Tel: 503–2408/9 and 503–2400.
Logan, Bernhard and Okamoto	330 New Otemachi Building, 4 Otemachi, 2-chome, Chiyoda-ku, Tokyo. Tel: 211–1721/3.
McIvor, Kauffman and Christenssen	Suite 729, New Tokyo Building, 2,3-chome, Marunouchi, Chiyoda-ku, Tokyo. Tel: 211–8871.
*Takashima, Fumio	Marunouchi-Yaesu Building, Room 322,2–6 Marunouchi, Chiyoda-ku, Tokyo. Tel: 281–0683.
*Usami Law Office	Room 319, Sanshin Building, 10,1-chome, Yurako-cho, Chiyoda-ku, Tokyo. Tel: 591–4716/7620, 3776.

*Yuasa, Sakamoto, Kawai and Ikenega	Room 206, New Otemachi Building, 4,2-chome, temachi, Chiyoda-ku, Tokyo. Tel: 270–6641.

*Members of the English Bar.

Source: Board of Trade, London

In doing business with Japan, prices should be quoted c.i.f., but it may also be helpful to list them f.o.b. It is quite satisfactory to quote in dollars or in sterling. The metric system should be used for weights and measures.

Most large Japanese firms have English-speaking personnel on their staffs, and it is permissible to use English in correspondence, as this has become the standard medium for conducting foreign trade in Japan. On the other hand, trade literature should be translated into Japanese. Usually, local agents can take care of this.

Any foreign visitor who requires the help of translation or interpreter services will have no problems in Japan. He can even arrange for the services of a licensed interpreter to become available to him immediately on arrival in the country, through his travel agency; or very quickly afterwards, by enquiring at the information desk of his hotel.

Translating and secretarial services

Nagashima Associates	Imperial Hotel, Tel: 591–3151, Ext 89.
I.S.S. Incorporated	Tokyo Prince Hotel, Tel: 434–4221, Ext 1460.
I.S.S. Incorporated	Tokyo Hilton Hotel, Tel: 581–4511, Ext 598/9.
Manpower	Chuo Daiwa Building, 13–13,1-Chome Ginza Chuo-ku, Tel: 562–4271.

Jack Yamashita Secretarial Service	6th Floor, Kaneda Building, 41 Naka-dori, 3-chome, Shibuya-ku, Tel: 409–1981.
Jack Yamashita Secretarial Service	Sixth Floor, Kaneda Building, 17–2, 3-chome, Shibuya-ku, Tel: 211–5211, Ext 214.
Okura Hotel Secretarial Service	Tel: 582–0111, Ext 292.
Japan Guide Association	Shin Kokusai Building, 3–4 Marunouchi, Chiyoda-ku, Tel: 213–2706.
*Tokyo Public Relations Service	1–7, 1-chome, Uchisaiwaicho, Chiyoda-ku, Tel: 571–0687.

*Translation service only.

Source: Board of Trade, London

Import policies

While in recent years Japan has been adopting more liberal policies on imports, several so-called sensitive items still are subject to licensing. In Japan, three main types of licensing are used, as follows:

Automatic Approval System	(AA)
Automatic Import Quota	(AIQ)
Import Quota	(IQ)

The AA type of licence applies to certain raw materials and semi-finished products, and even some manufactured goods, which are considered essential to the Japanese economy. Licences are usually automatically approved for such products on application directly to a Japanese Foreign Exchange Bank.

The AIQ system applies to imports of less essential

nature, but which are likely to receive favourable consideration, including, for example, many kinds of machinery. To obtain this type of licence, it is necessary to apply to the Ministry of International Trade and Industry for a foreign exchange certificate, valid for one month. The application should be accompanied by trade literature, price information and similar data. The certificate must then be exchanged for an import licence at a Foreign Exchange Bank during the period of validity. If the initial application is approved, subsequent applications, and the necessary foreign exchange, in principle are granted automatically.

The IQ system covers certain other types of capital goods, and such consumer goods as, for example, woollen textiles, leather footwear, whisky, confectionery, biscuits and other food items, which the Japanese authorities consider less essential. For approved items coming under the IQ system the Ministry of International Trade normally issues foreign exchange certificates valid for four months, which can be exchanged at a Foreign Exchange Bank, again so long as they remain valid. Such applications are considered on their merits.

When applying for any type of licence, an importer must make collateral deposits with the Bank, equal to a proportion of the merchandise involved. Rates are at present 1 per cent for raw materials and industrial machinery, and 5 per cent for most other goods. To obtain a refund, the importer must bring in at least 80 per cent of the amount for which the licence has been granted, normally within six months; otherwise, the deposit is forfeit.

With the exception of certain raw materials and essential industrial equipment, imports into Japan are subject to customs duty. The rate of duty usually represents a percentage of the price of the goods sold in wholesale quantity in the country of origin, plus the expenses of shipment, freight and insurance. The Japanese Customs Tariff uses the Brussels Nomenclature. Certain items enter at favourable rates under GATT or most favoured nation conventions.

Each import shipment must be accompanied by a certificate of origin, personally signed and dated, and containing such data as the place of origin, marks/ numbers and description of goods, number of packages, and quantity and value of the merchandise. Two copies of the commercial invoice are required, which should include the mark, number, description and value of the goods, the Brussels Nomenclature number, place and date of invoice, names and addresses of the consignor and consignee, and conditions of contract relating to the value of the goods.

For goods subject to *ad valorem* duties, the cost of packing, freight, insurance, commission, and any other shipping charges should be indicated. Invoices should be personally signed; pro forma invoices are rejected. Requirements for bill of lading are specified in the letter of credit, but in the regular way, three signed original bills are required by banking authorities, and at least two unsigned copies by the consignee.

Certificates of origin can be obtained at Japanese consulates abroad, but also are issued by customs authorities and chambers of commerce.

The import of merchandise in parcels into Japan is subject to the production of an import licence which can be obtained by the addressee. Parcels up to a maximum weight of 22 pounds (10 kilos) may be sent by surface or air transport. Samples to a value of 500 dollars (£210) or less normally can be imported without problems, on declaration to the customs authorities, provided the importer is using his own foreign exchange.

Articles taken into Japan for exhibition and demonstration may be imported free of duty and tax, provided they are to be re-exported within one year from the date of the import permit. To bring in samples of high value, it is necessary to make application to the Ministry of Trade and Industry.

Licensing

In some circumstances, the arrangement desired by the foreign firm in Japan may not be the straight agency connection, but, to take two other typical set-ups, a licensing or joint venture agreement with a local firm.

Conditions governing the licensing of technology have been liberalised in the country in recent years. Imports involving payment of 50,000 dollars (£21,000) or less related to technology licensing now are more or less automatically approved by the Bank of Japan. Above that figure, they also are usually allowed in, with the exception of certain sensitive fields, such as aircraft, petrochemicals and atomic power.

Government approval is usually needed for any joint venture in which foreign interests participate. The proportion of foreign capital permitted in such transactions very rarely is allowed to exceed 50 per cent, though regulations in this area also are being progressively relaxed.

Foreign firms are currently discouraged from setting up manufacturing operations in Japan, especially any that might threaten to damage local medium-sized or smaller business. Other branch operations, such as sales offices, are more favourably regarded. In considering all applications for licensing and joint venture agreements, the Japanese authorities are interested to know if these would permit exports to third markets.

Patents

The foreign firm which plans to export to Japan is advised to patent any inventions and register trade marks, in the country. Japan subscribes to the International Convention for the Protection of Industrial Property of 1934. Application for a patent can be made, either in the country of origin or in Japan, by the inventor or his assignee, which can be an individual, firm or corporation.

An application, other than a Convention application, should be filed before the invention has become publicly known or has been used in public in Japan, and before it has been described in any publication available to the public in any other country.

Patents are granted for a term of fifteen years from the date of publication of the application, subject to the payment of annual renewal fees, but in no case may the life of a patent extend beyond twenty years from the date of the application. If a patented invention is not worked in Japan for a period of three years or more, the patentee may be required to grant licences.

Trade mark registration extends for ten years in Japan, but may be cancelled if there has been no *bona fide* use of the mark for a period of three years. Application for renewal should be made not more than three months before expiration of the registration.

Publicity

Japan has three daily newspapers with nationwide mass circulation of more than 4 million for the morning, and 2·5 million for the afternoon editions. Ten or so of the 150 regional and local dailies have a circulation of over 250,000, and there is one daily business newspaper with one million morning and about half-a-million evening circulation.

Three morning and one evening newspapers, with a much more limited circulation, are published in the English language, chiefly read in the Tokyo-Yokohama and Osaka-Kobe areas. Also, the English-language daily, *Shipping and Trade News* contains considerable international business news.

All of these may prove suitable media for the advertising of foreign firms. Certain to prove valuable are the numerous trade magazines, which, however, are published in Japanese. One advantage is that their advertising rates are comparatively low.

So, too, are those of the Japanese broadcasting

stations, of which there are 150 or so, owned by fifty firms; though four in Tokyo dominate the television network of about 440 relay stations all over the country. These are equipped to handle colour TV broadcasts. Japanese cinemas, still much patronised, present commercial messages on slide and film.

Japan has a few large and influential advertising agencies, and, besides, the major United States and European agencies also nowadays have branches in the country. One type of promotional activity on which the Japanese themselves place great emphasis is the trade fair.

Throughout the year, general and special trade fairs and exhibitions are regularly staged, on a permanent basis, generally in Tokyo and Osaka. In addition, special exhibitions are frequently sponsored.

Advertising

Japanese advertising methods, once so badly out-dated, are today shaped by the country's close economic associations with the United States. The relationship— expressive of the frank admiration of Japan's business community for American efficiency—remains fairly solid but there is evidence that the avid student may be about to surpass the teacher. Millions of dollars worth of television advertising films and animated cartoons are sold each year to US advertising agencies on Madison Avenue by the Japanese. Most of Japan's leading printing houses would suffer profit decreases if they did not receive steady orders for art work from New York.

If recent trends continue, it may not be long before American advertising executives start to adapt some of Japan's more distinctive advertising ideas for use in the US. In the meantime, however, there are still respects in which Japan lags behind. The function of many Japanese advertisements is to attract attention to trademarks, company names or actual products—but not very often is the goal to actually sell.

Japanese advertisements seldom if ever include a direct command, such as 'Use Ponds Face Cream' or 'Drink Schweppes'. Television, radio, newspapers, magazines, billboards and direct mail or film advertisements make heavy use of personalities. Only since the mid-1960s have consumer goods manufacturers found advertisements really helpful in selling their products to the homogenous 100 million Japanese. It has been a difficult task to bring in customers by means of advertisements pushing the virtues of a certain item because the dynamic and imaginative Japanese still seem to feel that blowing your own trumpet shows a lack of humility. Although this is changing rapidly, probably due to the influence of such American agencies as J. Walter Thompson, Grant, McCann Erickson and others large enough to afford offices in Tokyo, there are still remarkable (and mysterious) differences.

To an unusual degree, Japanese advertising is controlled by the agencies who serve largely as advance space buyers and sellers, hawking their wares to customers, often without consideration of the requirement of a particular product message to reach a specific audience. This too is changing, much to the relief of the more sophisticated Japanese marketing specialists.

Well-thought-out advertising campaigns in Japan are mainly the products of the agencies employed by foreign corporations and it is quite common in Japan for domestic agencies to handle competitive accounts. Nevertheless, a surprising amount of local advertising is placed on behalf of foreign products.

The Japanese, however, have not often reaped the full benefits of their advertising efforts, contrary to the successes of foreign advertising campaigns. The major reason appears to be that in Japan it is still the rare advertising agency or client company which has a complete understanding of the part played by advertising in marketing. Certainly the quality of appreciation is not comparable with that of businessmen in Britain, West Germany, France and the United States. Often in Japan interbusiness relationships determine just how much will be spent on advertising and in some not unusual cases, how far the message will go in lauding qualities of the product.

Thus, instead of accepting foreign advertising as a challenge to be duplicated or surpassed, it is not unusual for Japanese competitors to complain to their local associates and eventually to protest to the fair trade commission that the foreign company is 'competing excessively' by making use of its 'over capitalisation'. This is unfortunate since the Japanese are beginning to take to advertising as a marketing tool and are not far from appreciating the magical advantages which can accrue to domestic firms.

Japanese advertising agency executives employ top visual technicians, some excellent copy-writers and an impressive psychological understanding of their marketing goal. Yet from time to time it is possible to see advertisements on TV or in various publications which are in unheard of bad taste or which have obviously missed the point. The ingredients have not been mixed properly in some cases, leaving the viewer uncomfortable at best. Lack of properly integrated advertising and marketing concepts is another problem causing confusion. Undoubtedly Japan's newly affluent society is not yet sufficiently sophisticated to demand improvements. It is the better advertising agencies themselves which are giving the situation the attention required to provide the depth of professional cultivation that should in the mid-1970s enable the nation's advertising to match the highest international levels.

38

Language

The structure of the Japanese sentence is generally the opposite of most European languages. Relative clauses precede and do not follow the noun they qualify. Verbs generally come at the end, and instead of prepositions Japanese has post-positions or particles which act as grammatical aids. For instance, an English sentence such as the following, 'Can you please tell me the way to the Mitsukoshi department store at Nihonbashi?' becomes something like this: 'Nihonbashi particle Mitsukoshi department store to going route particle (to show object) tell please?'. 'I have just finished reading a very interesting book which I bought at Maruzen bookstore yesterday' becomes something like this: 'Yesterday Maruzen called bookstore at bought book particle (to show object) just reading finished have.' This kind of sentence structure means that an interpreter cannot attempt to put only part of a sentence into Japanese and that in so-called simultaneous interpretation he cannot begin to interpret until he has heard at least a whole sentence.

USEFUL WORDS AND PHRASES—ENGLISH/JAPANESE

Good morning	OHAYO GOZAIMASU
Good day	KONNICHI-WA
Good evening	KONBAN-WA

Goodbye	SAYONARA
Good night	O-YASUMI NASAI
My name is . . .	WATASHI-NO NAMAE-WA . . . DESU
Glad to meet you	HAJIMEMASHITE
How are you?	IKAGA DESU-KA?
Excuse me	SHITSUREI SHIMASU
Do you know English?	EIGO-GA DEKIMAS-KA?
Do you understand?	WAKARI-MASU-KA?
I don't understand	WAKARI-MASEN
I am sorry	GOMEN-NASAI
Please	DOZO
Please wait a moment	CHOT'TO MAT'TE KUDASAI
Please say it again	MOO ICHIDO OS'SHAT'TE KUDASAI
Thank you	ARIGATO
Thank you very much	DO-MO ARIGATO GOZAIMASU
What time is it?	IMA, NAN'JI-DESU-KA?
YES	HAI
No	IIE
Good	YOI *or* II
Bad	WARUI
I must be going	SHITSUREI SHIMASU

Arrival

I should like to change some money	RYO'GAE SHITAI-NO-DESU- GA
Pound sterling	EIKOKU-PON'DO
Japanese yen	NIHON-EN
Where is the toilet?	TOIRET'TO-WA DOKO-DESU-KA?
Where can I get a taxi?	TAKUSHI-WA DOKO DESU-KA?
Please take me to this address	KONO JUSHO-MA'DE IT'TE KUDASAI
Please stop	TOMATTE KUDASAI

Dining

Please show me the menu	MENYU-O MISETE KUDASAI
What is the speciality of the house?	KOKO-NO JIMAN-NO RYORI-WA DORE DESU-KA?
The bill please	KANJO O KUDASAI
That is all, thank you	MO TAKUSAN-DESU
Thank you for the delightful meal	DOMO GOCHISO SAMA DESHITA

Shopping

How much is it?	IKURA-DESU-KA?
Please show me something else	HOKA-NO-O MISETE KUDASAI
I'll take this please	KORE O KUDASAI
I don't want it thank you	SUMIMASEN GA YAMETE OKIMASU
Please give me a receipt	UKETORI-O KUDASAI

Doctor

| Please call a doctor | ISHA-O YONDE KUDASAI |

Mail

I should like to send a telegram	DEMPO O UCHITAI NO DESU GA
Please send this letter by airmail	KONO TEGAMI-O KOKUBIN-DE DASHITAI NO DESU GA (or KONO TEGAMI-O KOKUBIN-DE DASHITE KUDASAI)
Please give me some picture postcards	EHAGAKI-O KUDASAI

Days of the week

Sunday	NICHIYO
Monday	GETSUYO
Tuesday	KAYO
Wednesday	SUIYO
Thursday	MOKUYO

Friday	KIN'YO
Saturday	DOYO

Numerals

One	HITOTSU
Two	FUTATSU
Three	MIT'TSU
Four	YOT'TSU
Five	ITSUTSU
Six	MUT'TSU
Seven	NANATSU
Eight	YAT'TSU
Nine	KOKONOTSU
Ten	TO

Months

January	ICHI-GATSU
February	NI-GATSU
March	SAN-GATSU
April	SHI-GATSU
May	GO-GATSU
June	ROKU-GATSU
July	SHICHI-GATSU
August	HACHI-GATSU
September	KU-GATSU
October	JU-GATSU
November	JU-ICHI-GATSU
December	JU-NI-GATSU

Days

Today	KYO
Yesterday	KINO
Tomorrow	ASU (or ASHITA)

The numerals given above are generally used when specifying how many of a certain article, e.g. in ordering drinks. When referring to numerals in words, e.g. giving hotel rooms or telephone numbers, the Japanese use a different series.

256

1	ichi		100	hyaku
2	ni		200	nihyaku
3	san		300	sambyaku
4	yon		400	yonhyaku
5	go		500	gohyaku
6	roku		600	roppyaku
7	nana		700	nanahyaku
8	hachi		800	happyaku
9	ku		900	kyuhyaku
10	ju		1,000	sen
20	niju		10,000	man
30	sanju		1,000,000	hyakuman
40	yonju		100,000,000	oku
50	goju		1,000,000,000,000	cho
60	rokuju			
70	nanaju			
80	hachiju			
90	kyuju			

The series can be continued simply by adding the integers to 10 and its multiples, thus 11 is juichi, 22 is nijuni, and so on. But ku becomes kyu in compound numbers.

Doing business—English/Japanese

Accountant	KAIKEI-KAKARI
advertising	KOKOKU
amortisation	NENPU-SHOKAN
assets	SHISAN
atomic energy	GENSHIRYOKU ENERUGI
Balance of payments (international)	KOKUSAI-SHUSHI
balance sheet	TAISHAKU TAISHO-HYO
bank rate	KOTEI BUAI
bankruptcy	HASAN
board (of directors)	YAKUIN-KAI (TORISHIMARI-YAKU-KAI)
boom	KO-KEIKI
Capital equipment	SHIHON-SETSUBI
cargo handling	KAMOTSU-SHORI

cash flow	GENKIN-RYUTSU
chairman	KAICHO
company	KAISHA
cost of living	SEIKEI-HI
consultant	CONSULTANT
consumer	SHOHI-SHA
consumer goods	SHOHI-ZAI
contract	KEI-YAKU
Data processing	DETA-SHORI
debt	FUSAI
Deposit	YOKIN
depreciation	GENKA-SHOKYAKU
development	KAIHATSU
director	TORISHIMARI-YAKU
managing director	SENMU (-TORISHIMARI- -YAKU)
discount	WARIBIKI
dividend	HAITO-KIN
Economy	KEIZAI
estimate	MITSUMORI
exchange rate	GAIKOKU-KAWASE SOBA
executive	KEI-EI SHA
Financial year	KAIKEI-NENDO (in Japan from April to March)
fixed assets	KOTEI SHISAN
forecasting	YOSOKU
foreman	SHOKU-CHO
freight	UN-CHIN
Growth rate	SEI CHO-RITSU
Hire purchase	SHIN-YO HANBAI
Income	SHOTOKU
industry	SANGYO
inflation	INFLATION
installation	SETSUBI

insurance	HOKEN
inventory	ZAIKO
investment	TOSHI
' invoice	INVOICE
Liabilities	FUSAI
liquidation	SEISAN
losses	KESSON
Machine tool	KOSAKU-KIKAI
management	KEI-EI
manager	SHIHAI-NIN
general manager	SO-SHIHAI-NIN
manufacturing	SEIZO
market	SHIJO
materials handling	GENRYO-SHORI
maturity	MANKI
merger	GAPPEI
Obsolescence	CHINPU-KA
order book	CHUMON-UKE-DAICHO
output	SEISAN-DAKA
overtime	JIKANGAI-RODO
overhead(s)	KOKYO-TOSHI
Patent	TOKKYO
packaging	HOSO
personnel	SHOKU-IN
profitability	RIEKI-SEI
public corporation	KOSHA
Quality control	HINSHITSU-KANRI
quota	WARI-ATE
Raw materials	GENZAIRYO
research	CHOSA
restrictive practice	SEIGENTEKI-KANKO
retail	KO-URI

Salary	KYURYO
sample	MIHON
shipment	SHUKKA
subsidiary	HOJOKIN
surplus	YOJO
Tax	ZEI
technical	GIJUTSU-NO
trade union	RODO-KUMIAI
trend	KEIKO
turnover	URIAGEKAKA (DEKIDAKA)
Unemployment	SHITSUGYO
Wage	CHINGIN
working capital	EIGYO-SHIHON
writing down	CHOBO-KAKAKU-NO-HIKISAGE

Linguaphone Institutes*

Australia	Linguaphone Institute, 45, Chandos Street, St Leonards, New South Wales
Belgium	Institut Linguaphone, CCI, 54, Rue du Midi, Brussels.
Brazil	Instituto Audio Visual e de Idiomas SA, Andradas 1428, Porto Alegre.
Denmark	Linguaphone Institutet A/S, Frederiksberggade 12, Copenhagen.

*For anyone wanting a quick, working knowledge of spoken Japanese, the Linguaphone Institute has a specially-designed course.

France	Centre Nobelia SA,
	12 Rue Lincoln,
	Paris, 8^e.
West Germany	Linguaphone Sprachkurse GmbH,
	Neuer Wall 42,
	2 Hamburg 36.
India	Linguaphone Institute,
	359, D. Naoroji Road,
	Bombay,1.
Italy	La Nuova Favella S.r.1,
	Via Borgospesso 11-15,
	Milan, 204.
Japan	Linguaphone Institute (Japan) Ltd,
	Tameike Meisan Bldg 1-12,
	1-chome,
	Akasaka,
	Minato-ku,
	Tokyo.
Singapore	Stamford College,
	72, The Arcade,
	Raffles Place (P.O. Box 281).
Sweden	Linguaphone Institutet,
	Kungsgatan 18,
	Stockholm.
Switzerland	Institut de Langues SA,
	16, Place Longemalle,
	1211 Geneva, 3.
Thailand	Praepittaya Co. Ltd,
	716/718, Burapa Palace,
	Bangkok.
United Kingdom	Linguaphone Institute,
	207/208, Regent Street,
	London, W1R 8AU.
USA	Linguaphone Institute,
	680, Fifth Avenue,
	New York, N.Y. 10019.

Book list

The Chrysanthemum and the Sword; Patterns of Japanese Culture by Ruth Benedict. A stimulating introduction to the traditional Japanese code. But the author never visited Japan, and things have changed since she wrote in the 1940s.

Things Japanese by B. H. Chamberlain. This 1905 classic has since been reprinted many times. Although much of it is out of date, the author knew Japan well, and has a dry sense of humour.

Japan Past and Present by Edwin O. Reischauer. The standard pocket history by a former U.S. Ambassador to Japan.

Meeting with Japan by Fosco Maraini. A personal and searching portrait of the country by an Italian lover of Japan.

A Portrait of Japan by Laurens van der Post. Photography by Burt Glinn. A beautifully produced picture book with a short but well observed text.

Japan's Economic Expansion by G. C. Allen. The latest in a series of works by a British authority on the Japanese economy.

Japan Economic Year Book published by the *Oriental Economist*.

Japan Travel Companion and other handbooks published by the Japanese Travel Bureau.

Industrial Review of Japan edited by the *Nihon Keizai Shimbun, Tokyo.*

Directory of Foreign Residents published by the *Japan Times.*

ENGLISH LANGUAGE NEWSPAPERS AND PERIODICALS

The Japan Times (daily).

The Japan Times Weekly.

The Japanese language papers *Asahi Shimbun* and *Mainichi Shimbun* also publish daily English language versions.

The *Nihon Keizai Shimbun,* the main economic daily paper, publishes a weekly English language edition called the *Japan Economic Journal.*

The Oriental Economist is a serious economic monthly devoted almost entirely to Japan.

The Far East Economic Review of Hong Kong, a weekly publication covering other Far Eastern countries as well as Japan.

Contributors

D. W. Anthony, Centre of Japanese Studies, Sheffield University.

Trevor Boon, Japan Light Machinery Centre, London.

Professor Geoffrey Bownas, Director, Centre of Japanese Studies, Sheffield University.

Mary Campbell, *Financial Times*.

Reginald Cudlipp, Director of Anglo-Japanese Economic Institute.

A. E. Cullison, *Financial Times* Correspondent, Tokyo.

Gordon Daniels, Centre of Japanese Studies, Sheffield University.

Sir John Figgess, K.C.M.G., Commissioner General for Britain at EXPO '70.

Robert Graham, *Financial Times*.

G. H. Healey, Centre of Japanese Studies, Sheffield University.

Christopher Johnson, Managing Editor, *Financial Times*.

Trevor T. Jones, Shell Centre, London.

James Mackay, British Museum.

David Morris, Anglo-Japanese Economic Institute.

Terry Noone, International Editor, *Electronics Weekly*.

Marvin Petal, Chief of Tokyo Bureau, *McGraw-Hill World News*.

Henry Scott Stokes, special contributor to the *Financial*

Acknowledgements

We are grateful to the following for permission to reproduce copyright material:

The Board of Trade for extracts from 'Hints to Businessmen Visiting Japan' and the 'Trading with Japan' booklets produced by the British Embassy in Tokyo; the author for an extract adapted from a speech, 'Japan Today—Some Effects of the New Affluence', delivered to the Royal Central Asian Society by Sir John Figgess; *The Financial Times* for extracts from their special supplement on Japan issued 22 September, 1969; Japan Air Lines Co. Ltd. for extracts from various publications; Japan Association for the 1970 World Exposition for the official cherry blossom symbol of EXPO '70 (EXPO 70–4–UO–14); Linguaphone Institute Ltd. for a list of the major countries in which Linguaphone Japanese courses are available and for the addresses of their respective institutes; *Management Today* for extracts from 'The Managers of Japan' by Rex Winsbury from the issue dated July 1969.

For permission to reproduce photographs and maps we are grateful to:

Architectural Review; Camera Press Ltd.; the *Financial Times;* Mr. Y. Futagawa; the Gulbenkian

Museum, University of Durham; Japan Information Centre, London; Japan National Tourist Organization; Japan Trade Centre, London; the Japanese Foreign Ministry; Mainichi Newspapers; *Nihon Keizai Shimbun; Der Stern;* the Victoria and Albert Museum, London.

We would also like to thank Mr. Soshichi Miyachi of *Nihon Keizai Shimbun* and the Embassy of Japan, London for their help in compiling this book.

These ideograms express in Japanese the title of this book.

躍進日本